Growing

Old

in Poetry

GROWING OLD IN POETRY

Two Poets, Two Lives

SYDNEY LEA

&

FLEDA BROWN

GREEN WRITERS PRESS *Brattleboro, Vermont*

Printed in the United States

10 9 8 7 6 5 4 3 2 1

Green Writers Press is a Vermont-based publisher whose mission is to spread a message of hope and renewal through the words and images we publish. Throughout we will adhere to our commitment to preserving and protecting the natural resources of the earth. To that end, a percentage of our proceeds will be donated to environmental activist groups and other social and environmental justice groups. Green Writers Press gratefully acknowledges support from individual donors, friends, and readers to help support the environment and our publishing initiative.

GReen
wrITers
press

Giving Voice to Writers Who Will Make the World a Better Place
Green Writers Press | Brattleboro, Vermont
www.greenwriterspress.com

ISBN: 978-0-9994995-5-9

COVER IMAGE:
Three Medlars with a Butterfly, Adriaen Coorte, 1705,
oil on paper mounted on panel, 27 cm (10.6 in) x 20 cm (7.9 in)

PRINTED ON PAPER WITH PULP THAT COMES FROM FSC-CERTIFIED FORESTS, MANAGED FORESTS THAT GUARANTEE RESPONSIBLE ENVIRONMENTAL, SOCIAL, AND ECONOMIC PRACTICES BY LIGHTNING SOURCE. ALL WOOD PRODUCT COMPONENTS USED IN BLACK & WHITE, STANDARD COLOR, OR SELECT COLOR PAPERBACK BOOKS, UTILIZING EITHER CREAM OR WHITE BOOKBLOCK PAPER, THAT ARE MANUFACTURED IN THE LAVERGNE, TENNESSEE PRODUCTION CENTER ARE SUSTAINABLE FORESTRY INITIATIVE® (SFI®) CERTIFIED SOURCING.

ACKNOWLEDGMENTS

THE AUTHORS WOULD LIKE TO thank the editors of the following periodicals, in which many of these essays, sometimes in slightly or even radically different form, first appeared:

Numéro Cinq, New Ohio Review, Northern Woodlands, The Georgia Review, Stymie, Brevity, New England Review; Sydney's "Prelude" appears also in his book, *A North Country Life.*

CONTENTS

INTRODUCTION

THE FIRST-EVER CONFERENCE for state poets laureate was held in Manchester, New Hampshire in 2003. Thirty-eight laureates, from all over the country, participated in panel discussions and presentations, but they also fanned out across the state to give readings. Syd was Fleda's companion and guide for the readings, offering a poem or two of his own at each venue before ceding the lectern to her as Delaware's then poet laureate. We read together, for example, at a small café in Whitefield, nestled deep among the White Mountains, and at a retirement home in North Haverhill on the banks of the Connecticut River. Remembering the latter event, Fleda wrote this prose poem:

Reading Poetry at the Horse Meadow Senior Center

We'd been told fish for lunch, so we took bets on how it would be cooked and I guess I won, although we couldn't be sure if it was baked or broiled under the sauce, which, being guests, we pushed around against the spinach. Not true: some of us ate, including Syd, who lived nearby and said don't joke, he might be here someday, and we were all

scanning tables, seeing our own bodies rounding back to creation, our exact and precious sufferings slowly leaking out. The beached whale of poetry, I thought, not seeing Syd but myself, exhausted into prose. Syd got up, as directed, postscrod and pre-cobbler, so people wouldn't drift away, and he read a poem that played up the local, and then I pulled

the mike toward them as far as the cord went, using my old joke about the end of my rope, and they laughed, and I started with a poem about my daughter that seemed to end right. Then I read "Dock" because of its repetition, so they wouldn't

miss rhyme too much, that elephant in the room. I had time
between to think of Longfellow, the way

"shining big sea waters" lies off in the varnished distance
and leaves a person free afterward to take a nap. Then I read
the one about my grandfather forgetting where he was and
thought halfway through, uh-oh, but they smiled and clapped,
sure of where they were, and by this time those who wanted it
had finished a second dish of peach cobbler

and I felt really happy, useful, part of the general flow of
things. I felt like a closing line myself, made of nothing but
words intended to swim out into the stratosphere, but caught,
luckily, among the wheelchairs and walkers.

(from *Reunion*, University of Wisconsin Press, 2007)

We saw that we both cared a great deal about relating to our
audiences, no matter their makeup, indeed the less "specialized"
the better; we believed in offering them poems that might help
them make sense of their lives, just as composing them performed
that service for us. Such a notion of poetry's mission remains a
key aspect of our affection for and understanding of one another.

We've only been together in person a few times since, as when
Fleda came to the Frost Place in Franconia, New Hampshire to
teach and read, or at the 2009 AWP convention in Denver. But in
spite of the geographical distance that separates us, we've become,
perhaps oddly, deep, good friends, trading poems and thoughts
and worries and hopes and stories for all these years by email.

We are about the same age, we've each published a pile of books,
we've each retired from long university careers, we each have
families we love, we each have been, or are, poets laureate of our
states. We're each grumpy about some of the same things. We
greatly admire one another's poetry.

We suspect old-timer poets, our spiritual kin, may identify and
commiserate with what we say here—or better, celebrate it. And for
those who don't write poetry, these essays may be windows into a

life in poetry. Are poets' lives any different in tone or texture from other sorts of life?

Above all, though, we hope this book will be useful for young poets interested in knowing what a life in poetry may entail: What does it look like from the ground floor? How does one build it by way of attention to detailed experiences like ones that the book chronicles? We've been vain enough to imagine value in portraying how one man and one woman stumbled their ways toward poetry, which has been sometimes a moat in the eye, sometimes a beacon. We'd like to think our joy in the making of poetry is evident, and perhaps even contagious.

And of course, our book is a record of an important friendship.

—S.L. and F.B.

GROWING

OLD

IN POETRY

PRELUDES

— Syd

HOOKUM-SNUFFIE. Almost no one knows what it means anymore, and few would care.

Why on earth should they?

Everything about me, I have lately realized, is out of date, perhaps even more so than with most people of a certain age. Not much after dawn today, for instance, I took my straight ash paddle, fashioned by the late Hazen Bagley, and set out on the water in my wood and canvas canoe, fabricated by the Old Town Company, as closely as I can discover, in about 1950. I inherited the boat from my late father's late brother. Those two men took their sons way north in that boat and its 20-foot partner, my father's, which blew away some years later in a hurricane to the south of us. I was ten years old on that trip.

Those guide model canoes were more than merely beautiful. The hull planks were feathered, not butted, so that sand and grit could not get into their jointry. The fabled Grand Lake canoe-maker "Pop" Moore called them among the best such craft ever made.

A few hours back, my uncle's canoe glided me to the foot of the Machias River, its progress as smooth as the lake itself. To one like me, of course, there is far more inscrutable technology at work nowadays than ever went into a first-rate canoe. What can it mean, even out here, to be such a paddler in an era of jet skis, and perhaps more daunting, of internet service even at the summit of Mt. Everest?

What does solitude signify anymore? What is a writer of any kind, never mind a poet? Who are his readers? What on earth is a poet-woodsman, a poet-angler, a poet-hunter? Will he have any readers at all? If so, this is for them, and for all the superannuated men and women I'll be conjuring.

You cut a small branch of hardwood and then you fashion a hook by nipping it at a fork. With it you can lift a seething pot by its bale once your spuds or beans get to boiling over, or whenever they're ready to taste. That's the hookum. If you know what you're doing, you can judge the food's readiness by smell. That's the snuffie.

Hookum-snuffie: it's believed to derive from Pasamaquoddy pidgin, and no, it can't mean anything now. Still I say it. There's something deep in the word, and in many old others, that I always wanted, and want still, which is why I now and then make a hookum-snuffie, and why I never shape one without naming it aloud in the woods or on the shore and thereby seeing people I knew, people I was lucky to know, the last of the genuine woodsmen and their strong, valiant wives, who had their own equal, obsolete skills. 19th century figures, really.

I have come back and back to this corner of Maine for the great majority of my 75 years. Its hold on me grows even more powerful in the absence of those great persons I met in my young life. The hold is acuter as the part of me that busts the puckerbrush for wild birds or wades heavy water for trout or portages more than a few hundred yards sensibly weakens. Every joy in every game bird pointed and flushed, in every noble buck whitetail, every loon and moose and northwest wind, with its wild tattered apron of waves and its rushing clouds—every such elation here is at least equally freighted with its opposite. How can I surrender all this to others, few of whom can possibly know this region's history, as I do, by way of its characters?

I ache to see that foxfire glint again in dear Earl Bonness's eyes as he tends his flame and smutted cookware. He'll speak of felling great pines on Mopang Stream. I heard him talk. I yearn for George MacArthur, who could throw a broad-blade sleeper axe and bury it, time after time, in the trunk of some not-so-near tree. I saw him do it.

George and Earl always said they liked to work. Few now would likely imagine genuinely savoring the sort of labor that would kill them, as it would have me, even when I was twenty: pay by the job, not the hour.

The male old-timers are barrel-chested, deep-voiced figures, who still seem mythological, despite the tempering irony of my older man's vision. Earl knew what it was to ride the big logs over the rips clear down to the ocean, where they'd be gathered into big-sailed schooners and carried south to busier ports. George knew what it was to cut ties all one winter on White's Island without once seeing the camp in daylight. Out of it by lantern before dawn, back the same way after dark. George's niece Annie knew what it was to use a canoe for a dormitory, she and her husband Bill lacking a place to stay otherwise in the first summer of their marriage.

And I—I know what they told me.

They're long dead now. Everyone else in the world, or so it can seem in self-pitying, irrational moments, lies dead too.

The lumber company blew up the dam some forty years back, after moving timber by water was outlawed. Reaching the dam's ghostly site, I heard an eagle scream from her nest uplake. I started a fire and waited till the pot-lid danced. I hadn't even brought food to cook, only coffee. Hookum-snuffie, I breathed, imagination transforming those pillars of mist that trod water out on the lake in earliest morning. If I squinted my eyes, they looked like river drivers.

2017. The new century isn't all that hell-fired new anymore, though how recently it seemed so. Now it recedes into one before and one before that and words call to me, and phrases: deer noise on the beach, are gone on the clean jump; a tin cup wants more coffee; there are bad doings on the lake; a great felled tree is quite a stick...

Earl has a habit of tamping his pipe as he starts to spin a story. George makes a certain wave of his hand when he does: Do you mind the time, he begins, the verb an old form of remember. ...

It's as though I mind Earl making his way up the Mopang in his own canoe with a setting pole, standing. George spits on his chopping mitts before swamping a spot to drop the first big cedar.

Yes, I've long referred to myself as a poet, and though I do so in my late sixties with a satisfaction that diminishes as my sense of the art's future darkens, I don't quite know how else to know things. I still work at a magic return of what's vanished, that old profusion of a beloved idiom, one that lies hidden and hurts me. Language should save me, I seem to insist. I act as though it may, even though it must always fail, the failure sometimes greater and sometimes lesser.

Hookum-snuffie. I muttered. Then I doused my fire, steam wasting itself in the heavens. I said it again, slowly, as though a word—fossilized, forgotten—could quell longstanding desire.

PRELUDES

— *Fleda*

So, Syd, this is to be an elegy we're writing? I suppose all writing is elegy, all of it is powerful emotion recollected in tranquility. Don't we all start in on elegy—writers or not—at about age 13, when the gap begins to reveal itself to us, the sense of having an irretrievable past—our childhood—as well as a present, which holds what's already coming into being? The forward stroke of anticipation, the backward stroke of memory and nostalgia. When anticipation wears thin, as it does for us at our age, there starts to be more of the other. Or, the present is so infused with the past, it's hard to say which is which.

I walk down to the dock barefoot on the sandy soil under the cedars and hemlocks, carrying my towel. It's still so cool—65 degrees—that I dread the water, but you need to know, this is part of it, the dread that holds within it the joy of shock, the anticipation. Mist is still rising from the gradually-more-visible lake, one of those perfect days when I'll be the only disturbance on an otherwise still glimmer. I hang my towel on a stub of a tree branch, step off the dock into the water, and straight in, up to my neck, not pausing. If I give myself time to think, I'm lost. Or at least I spend more time agonizing over it. This way, when I'm in, I'm in.

I have a silly technique I think I've inherited from my father. As soon as my body is submerged, I breathe loudly, in short gasping breaths a few times as if I were a snorting horse. Somehow this absorbs the shock. It's a sound that registers both the enormity of the transition and my willingness to endure it.

I head south, in the direction of the yellow raft I use as a marker for where to turn around. I'm doing a leisurely breast stroke/frog kick combination I learned from my aunt Cleone, who learned it from her father, my grandfather, who learned it from a book when they first bought the cottage in 1919. It keeps the head above water, a friendly stroke that lets you talk to a friend while you both swim. It also keeps the hair dry, which is warmer. After the first three or four strokes, there is about five minutes of pure bliss, when the body feels with every nerve-ending the glassy slide of the water, no longer cold, maybe a bit numb, but perfect somehow.

I have no friend here this morning. I am the only one in the seven-mile long lake, I'm sure. Not just the only one in this early, but the only one really swimming, just to be swimming, all day. There will be the children playing with their plastic toys, the occasional quick dip of a few adults, and the stranded paddling of the ones who've fallen on their water skis as they wait for the boat to circle back around. Once I saw a couple of swimmers in wetsuits criss-crossing the lake like machines. One came close enough to the dock for me to ask. They were practicing for a triathlon.

So there are "professional" swimmers and there are those who splash around a bit. There are the professional writers, as you and I have been, and those, as we've also been, who splash around a bit. If I have to choose one, I guess I'd pick the splasher. I'll be a splasher who's learned how to do that well. In the water, most people plow across the surface by means of fierce motors, or edge across it with trolling motors, or zip around in circles on whiny jet skis that send huge rooster-tails flying behind for no more reason than the zipping around. Not that I object to having fun.

When I was a teenager, I wanted to go fast and make noise. I wanted to escape my childhood, who doesn't? We crawl, we toddle, we walk, and we learn to run. We see that motors take us even faster. We learn to drive. We want to win something out there that speed might get us closer to. We discover email. Okay, this is the way of the world.

I must be a dinosaur. I am pretty sure I am, out here in the water at 7 A.M., for no reason other than that I like it. A man in a fishing boat spots me. It takes him a minute to realize there's a real live person in the water. He waves and I do the same. I am probably that woman who swims in the morning. I remember Ted Metcalf swimming by our dock every day, barely above water, like grandfather, just slowly rising and falling into the little waves, basically a wave himself.

We come out of the slow waters of the womb, our natural habitat. Gradually, or not so gradually, our minds speed up, have sped up. At what point does the mind lift dangerously off the ground? At what point do we begin to live somewhere else, in a world invented by our minds, a world inside the cell phone, inside the computer?

I've been studying Buddhist texts. The Buddhists had 2500 years of looking at how all this works, how we lift off into the stratosphere and begin to feel this disconnect in our bones, this sense somehow we're not completely "here." They describe it in awesomely precise terms:

Our minds get to moving too fast, faster than nature moves. The mind gets a bit separated—a split second of "ignorance"—from reality. Instead of just living inside our reality, we're suddenly aware that we're being aware. Adam and Eve scramble for their clothes. This happened once, maybe, in human development, and it continues to happen each moment.

Oh my, something is aware! So, there must be a "someone," it looks like, to be aware. We get scared that the "someone" may not really exist, or that it will go away. We become desperate to hold onto this so-called solid self. We need something to keep us from this new feeling of aloneness, of having been tossed out of the garden. This is the first moment of elegy, isn't it?

If I were at this moment really neck deep in the lake, do you think I'd be going on about this, trying to keep this all straight in my mind? No way. I'd be swimming. I'd be alone, true, but happy. I think people need to think things through, develop systems and schemes, when the loneliness gets to them, when they're feeling like there's a place to get back to, one that was better, happier, somehow more "real" than now.

When the mind begins to make things "real," the karmic chain begins. We begin elaborately proving to ourselves that the "someone out there" is real: I "feel" this, therefore I am. I begin pushing and pulling, rattling the bars to prove I exist.

Thus begins the elaborate radar system to protect our sense of solid self: "No jet skis here! I hate them. I'll get rid of them." If there is an evil "not-me," there certainly must be a virtuous "me." Polemics! Politics!

Not-me/ me. I begin categorizing all the things that my mind is separating out. This is the intellect. Then, voilà, there's consciousness—my thoughts and emotions become my ego's army, constantly busy ratifying my existence. I am living in a cyberspace of ego, one I dreamed into being.

"Our birth is but a sleep and a forgetting," wrote Wordsworth 2,300 years after the Buddha.

Does the world not exist, then? Does our "past" exist? Probably not in the way we used to think. Contemporary physics tells us that what we thought was separate, isn't. And anyway, what are we? Every thread of our existence depends upon another thread. From this way of looking, to imagine we're separate beings is a dream.

I dream a lot of different things while I'm swimming along, stroke by easy stroke. My mind isn't entirely immersed in water.

It's wondering if what I see lifting out of the mist way up ahead is a person on a stand-up paddleboard—maybe someone other than me owns one, now!—or just a swim buoy. I'm remembering swimming here with my aunt Cleone, my sister Millie, my cousin Alan, my mother and father. I'm thinking of what to cook for supper. I'm thinking I forgot to call and change my dental appointment. I'm thinking how I will write this. But I am swimming, and a substantial part of my being is deep into it, enchanted, aware of the stroke, of the glide of water on my skin, of the position of my chin just under, the coordination of kick and stroke.

In *The Windward Shore*, Jerry Dennis's dazzling book of ruminations on wintering on the Great Lakes, he writes that our sense of enchantment has never left us, that it "occurs whenever the gap between us and what we encounter closes, making us forget ourselves and enter a connection with something or somebody else. It is the participating consciousness of the creative person, arrived at through involvement, engagement, the absorbed state, and to which the sense of wonder is a consequence that feels like a reward."

It is the gap that first opened—the fall from Paradise—that all art, all religion, all our elegizing, all our brave swimming in the soup of our immediate lives, longs to close. William Blake saw that we have to pass through innocence into experience in order to arrive, if that's the right word, at a higher innocence, a place where we bring everything with us—our possibly erudite learning as well as our clumsy beginnings, our successes and our failures. And when everything is with us, nothing is left to perceive a gap. No gap exists.

We keep this possibility as a longing, a memory.

It's hard to remember not being able to swim. I think I remember my aunt Cleone holding me loosely, one arm under my belly, while I practiced getting the frog kick coordinated with the arm movement. I can feel my impatience, my embarrassment when

I sank, my frustration. I'm not that much different, now, when it comes to learning new things. I wanted to know how to swim, but not to learn how. But it was time. I wouldn't be allowed to continue wearing the bulbous orange life jacket. I sank, I floundered, I swam. Then I was allowed the rowboat out alone, then. I got to swim across the lake with the adults. We all swam across the lake now and then, a caravan of swimmers, before the speedboats made it necessary to be accompanied by a canoe or kayak to call attention to us.

It's a mile to town by water. The story goes that back when everyone arrived by train, my grandparents had a guest arrive, and because his suitcases plus the groceries bought in town plus my grandparents and the guest were too much for the canoe—or rowboat, the story doesn't specify—my grandfather jumped in the lake and swam beside the boat all the way back to the cottage. I should mention that my grandfather had had TB, that had welded his ball and socket joint together on one leg, and he limped all his life, but to watch him swim was to hold one's breath. He preferred the "trudgeon" to the breast stroke for distance. He'd sink so low with each stroke, he seemed to be drowning. Then arm over, and head roll, and another stroke.

Both my grandparents swam close to a mile most days, across the narrow lake at an angle, toward Snowflake, a spiritualist camp, or toward town—physically, tangibly part of their environment. And my aunt Cleone. Her last few years, she'd come swimming with us and the cold would enter her thin old body so deeply that she'd shake so much all morning she could barely hold a tea cup. Even when I dried her long hair with my hair dryer. But she swam until she couldn't remember the lake, the stroke, her own life.

Before we had running water at the cottage—which was only a few years ago—we all swam before breakfast. We'd wash our hair in the lake and clean up for the day. No one thought much about leaving a residue of shampoo in the water. So much lake, so few people. All clothes-washing, though, was done in tubs and the water poured out way up the hill, to let it filter through the ground. These days we wouldn't have to worry about shampoo because no one washes her hair in the lake. No one does much of anything IN the lake. Things are done TO the lake. Zebra mussels are emptied into the lakes from ship ballast, and they make their way to the smaller lakes. Fertilizer runoff from lakeside lawns breeds algae. Water sloshes and erodes the banks all summer, from steadily churning boat propellers.

Today—the day I'm living in my head, the one I'm writing about, that in a way is also about writing, the day that is absolutely real and did and does exist within an eternity of possibilities—I come out of the water only a little chilled, my body still heated by its work in the water. It'll be half an hour before the chill sinks in and I start shivering, and put on my old brown sweater to bring me back up to temperature. I gather a few logs for the fireplace. But at the moment, my skin is part water, part air, immersed in the vast intelligence of water and air and mind. My small little mind confirms it, as if it needed to. Most of the time it thinks I live elsewhere and need to go to a lot of trouble longing for the past, when all I really have to do is light a fire, put on my sweater, and pour another cup of coffee.

BOOKS

Fleda—Books Made of Paper

T HE OLD LIBRARIES WERE UPSTAIRS. Up long, narrow stairs.
Maybe not all of them, but some. The one I knew. As if it
were a secret, a garret. They were all musty. Or some of them. Or,
the only one I knew back then, with its severe guardian, or one
who seemed severe, who had severe bones and counted the books
to the limit of six. When you're small, I suppose the world itself
outside of family feels severe, rule-bound, alien. But what do I
know of what it was like for others? I would climb the dark stairs
on Saturdays to where they opened out into the grand, narrow
stacks, and I would meander my way among them, not a clue what
I wanted, how to choose, except by heft, texture, print. All the
covers were red, green, or brown cloth-like texture on hardboard
of some sort, all the titles pressed into the board in black or gilt,
all worn. I think of everything as worn, the floors, the stacks
themselves, the central desk. I was entering a privacy, a sanctum
with hidden grottos, secrets. All that I did not know felt like an
emptiness in my skinny body. What I could know was stacked and
turned away, spines out, forbidding, colluding, pulling at me. I was
helpless and hopeless, and when I picked out my six, I had no idea
if they were the right ones. If they were the ones that would reveal
to me any part of what I needed for my soul.

Before that, I remember nothing of libraries. I remember story
hour in Middlebury, all of us hanging up our snowsuits and sitting
in a circle. I remember the circle but not the stories. How was it

that the stories went into me and lodged somewhere unreachable yet sent their perfume into the crevices of my character? I remember the semicircle of first grade, sounding out syllables one by one to hear the ruckus when Dick and Jane chased Spot around the yard. "No, Spot!" Jane called when the leaf pile flew into the air, pictures and words speaking in unison. I can smell the perfect certainty of the book, the waft of its origin, of organic matter. I can feel its soft, cloth-like pages with their slight sheen.

What did I read, after I could? Mostly easy books, below my level, for a long time. I was a lazy child in that way, wallowing alone in my own mind, wanting my mind separate, I guess, from the struggles toward a book's difficult language, difficult plot. I read and re-read Gertrude Chandler Warner's *The Boxcar Children,* my favorite book in grade school, the story of orphaned children who set up their home in a boxcar, who made it theirs by collecting cracked dishes from a nearby dump, dipping water from a convenient stream, going into town only to work briefly for a few potatoes, a little bread. I loved the way they distrusted the adult world's ability to look after them and went at it for themselves. I loved their small world. Home was a miniature windowless island on rusted rails on the outskirts of so-called civilization. I also loved *The Good Master,* by Kate Seredy, the story of a smart and wild Hungarian girl who was partially tamed by her kind uncle. I look it up, now. Amazon has copies in a new cover, but Wikipedia shows the original heart-shape on a blue background. It is only that version that I want. With the jacket a little frayed from use. But it's long gone, and even if I could have an exact replica, or the original bought from some used book dealer, I would not. It's the one on our cottage shelves that I want. It is the nine-year-old reading it over and over on long summer days that I want. Not me now. And Heidi. Another wild girl noticed and loved into good behavior by her kind uncle. Later when my friends were reading *Black Beauty;* I was being a horse, galloping across the playground. But not reading the stories. I read the Hardy Boys, some of them. I read Nancy Drew, some of them.

What I remember rather than stories themselves is the feel of reading. The way the book and I came together as if we were enclosed under gauze netting, the outside world barely whispering. I remember the graininess, the slightly darkened paper, the words actually pressed into them, the texture of the pressing. My body curled, holding in the story. When I was a teenager, my grandparents gave me a stack of old *Readers' Digest Condensed* books. I read them all, one after the other, lying in bed on summer mornings, lying in bed the month I had mono and had to stay home from school. Easy reading. Lazy.

It was as if my mind was needed elsewhere, to just live, to figure out my own life, to muddle through the day-by-day. All I could afford was this small turning away, this coasting into the heart of someone else's life. Through high school, I read what I had to—history, the sterile excerpts in my English anthology, I'm not sure what else. Nothing stands out. Even the most modest of writers' memoirs typically tout a list of books read by high school that I hadn't even heard of until mid-college.

Ah, college. I should mention I got myself married before I even set foot in the door of college. That's another story. But within that new stability, that safety, a wide and unforseen world began to present itself. My freshman reading list drove me wild with terror and joy. All I remember is that there were many pages in small type. Dickens, Camus, Tolstoy, maybe. One Christmas holiday, I read *War and Peace*, page by gloriously laborious page. I have a memory of reading it under a tree in the warmth of a winter afternoon in Arkansas, the snow of Moscow all around me.

Maybe we love what we love because it's hard going. Maybe we love it because we're supposed to. Maybe we don't love it at all, but want to prove something to ourselves. All I know is that my mind quivered with new ideas, with ratification of old ones, with the sheer physical weight of other people's words I cradled like a baby in my arms back and forth to class. I don't remember any back packs. Girls cradled their books and notebooks, stacked in their arms like a baby up to the chin. Boys carried them in one arm alongside. Knowledge had heft and weight, it pressed itself onto the page, it spread itself and turned itself in the breeze like leaves.

Meaning was an amalgam of the physical object: the book, its cover, its pages, and where the words flew into my mind and rearranged themselves according to the whims of my nature. I think it is not the grand and classic narrative, the movement of events, that held the meaning, but the feeling, the interstices, the spaces when I looked up from the page, where I stopped to scribble, and where, later, I brought along a whiff of what was there, to permeate my thoughts.

I am very visual, more than anything, and I would—and still do—recall what the page looks like, how far down the page, whether octavo or verso, where the lines I love appear. Their meaning has to do with font, with ink, with crispness, delicacy, or heaviness of the paper itself. The Norton anthologies with their biblically thin pages, the *Boxcar Children* with its sturdier ones, my Scotch-taped college copy of Chief Modern Poets of Britain and America, where D.H. Lawrence's "Whales Weep Not!" begins almost at the bottom of a page and fills up the next one. Where "urgent" and "urge" and "ice-bergs" are circled, with the note in the top margin, "[incantatory], and, and, and," holding my younger and excited self on the page forever. At the top margin of Robert Graves' poems, "always the practical impossibility, transcended only by miracle, of absolute love continuing between man and woman." My hand, Graves's words, Miller Williams' quoting them in class. Each part of a whole, a meaning. Yeats' "Second Coming," my ink drawing of a gyre, one triangular whirlwind on top of the next, with the note, "most rests upon A Vision, cataclysm every 2000 years."

The number of marks on a page is a measure of how engaged I am. Pen or pencil doesn't matter. For my husband, an Eighteenth Century scholar, books are sacred artifacts, or something close. He will not dog-ear a page of a book or mark it (except back when he was teaching), even when it's a cheap paperback. For him, it's respect for the tradition of the book, for the author, for the paper. I, however, want to mark how my mind is moving in and out of the author's mind. I think of our work as a partnership, and my role involves scribbling in margins. In a novel with a strong plot, I mark nothing, my mind dutifully, practically, racing forward.

On the Kindle, it is possible to underline sections, and then call them up, along with the relevant passages. You can then click on those and return to the page on which they appeared. Very convenient. You can take notes, only that is harder. You have to type them in on the little keypad. I bought a Kindle. I use it for maybe a quarter of my reading. I like being able to summon books from the ether and have them magically appear. I appreciate not having so many ephemeral paperbacks pile up that I have to figure who to give them to afterward. The print is good on the Kindle: neat serifs, soft background. No doubt whole committees have scientifically assessed the brightness of the screen, the font, the movement of the eye. Good job.

As my eye moves down the Kindle "page," I am aware of the words as barely being there, disappearing with a click to the next page, gone forever if I remove the book from my device. I feel the futility of saving anything, and interestingly, therefore, I begin to view my mind as the repository, rather than the bookshelf. I am my own bookshelf. And of course even I can't hold on to much. My mind is slippery and unreliable, unlike the firm book between covers. Unlike the world I imagined existed, the permanent one in the past, the better one, with manners, with tact, with grace and a clear list of what the well-read person has on her shelves.

I love the actual book. I am okay with the Kindle. What's lost, what's gained is hardly worth talking about because what's here is here and won't go away. Humans will always find the shortest path, given a chance. I just downloaded my first book of poems: Jane Hirshfield's *Come, Thief*. I'd heard poetry was a formatting problem for e-books, but this one seems fine, if sterile. I will probably use the Kindle mostly for fiction that I intend to get rid of later.

A poem cries out for paper, in my mind. It wants to be located, pinned down. I'm fine hearing a poem spoken or read, but I want to know it resides, at last, on what is for me its native habitat, the page. Why else the fuss with line endings, with indentations, with stanza breaks? Why else do poets argue with their publishers about fonts and point size? Of all genres, it seems that poetry most wants to be read simultaneously by eye and mind.

There's nothing more or less "real" about the words on Kindle versus the words pressed onto paper. The words themselves are not real. They're metaphors for what we "see" (also not "real") as we read. I could deconstruct all the way down, but everybody knows that. What matters is the relationship with meaning that each insinuates.

Someday this conversation is going to be so dated! Who cares if the molecules form themselves into pixels or press themselves into ink? What difference did it make when Gutenberg began pressing one after another pages, each a copy of the first? Was the work less authentic, being no longer in the delicate script of the copier? Are stone hieroglyphs "better" than print, being more permanent, more solid?

I am the generation who's been knocked on its tail by the systematic unmooring of all we held sacred. Never in human history has the past disappeared so quickly while at the same time remaining perpetually with us in film and TV. Our first little black and white Zenith TV entered our home when I was 13, my first computer when I was 40. After a traumatic struggle, I learned to love the word as it flashes at me from my screen. I love it on the page, I love it flying around in the air. I am a convert, mostly.

At the same time, I'm sad. I think only those of us who were young in a different world know what it is to move more slowly within it, to feel its edges as unrelenting rather than as possessing the infinite regress of the screen. To walk up the many steps to the library, its elevation a signifier of the invisible grandeur of its holdings—even the word "holdings" both warm and forbidding—pull open the long wooden card catalog drawers and run our finger along the cards softened by years of our predecessors, miss the right card, look again and find it! And write down the call numbers on a scrap of paper with a stub of a pencil, then stand in the crevasse between stacks letting our eye travel until—there it is!—our book. By now it is our book only, the one we looked for with our hands and feet and eyes, and found. The one chosen from the long, skinny drawer of cards. This one. The librarian stamps the borrower's card and slips it into the pocket at the back of the book. We can read who else has checked out the book. The names remain until that card is full and has to be replaced. Oh, this book hasn't been checked out in six years! How smart we are to have re-discovered it! We carry it home, place it on the table, and open it, the end of one journey, the beginning of another.

Not that people don't still do this. But when it was the only way, it seemed more important. Even the book felt somehow more necessary, a lifeboat in a storm, a lone squeee of a radio signal in the wilderness. When each book went through several printings, we could trace that in the front matter, and marvel at how many people must have read it. People. That's what I mourn, I guess. The thumbprint, the smudge, the marginal note, the hand that works the press. The hand, its slow and sometimes clumsy articulations. The universe is slow, really. The sun takes its own sweet time coming up and going down, tides come and go with time enough between for a sand castle to be built. No matter that it will be washed away. It was something: tall, many crenellated, gritty, its doors and windows made of our own fingerprints. It was right out of King Arthur. You could see the knights crossing the moat-bridge, clamoring their way right out of the book.

RE: BOOKS

Syd—What Will Suffice

Yes, COME TO THINK OF IT, dear Fleda, there seems something physical about the way books have figured into my life too; but that physicality may be pretty eccentric, and certainly not in a fashion to which the incomprehensible-to-me arrangement of electrons, the stuff of our incomprehensible-to-me techno age, feels relevant.

Or is my sense of self, archaic as it may be, so much mere vanity? Aren't we all eccentrics, poets no more than others? Perhaps the myth of our individuality is based on a more general myth, without which our treasured selfhood couldn't exist in the first place: namely that there's some "center" to be found out there in the human throng, from which we have somehow divagated, as the very etymology of the word eccentric suggests. It may be mere solipsism that allows an artist to apply such a term and such a concept to him- or herself and not, say, to the neighbor dentist or plumber or landscaper or physics professor.

Whatever the truth, and however crucial books have been and remain to my own version of the eccentric, I was quite emphatically not a bookish boy. The woods and fields of my bachelor uncle's farm were my encyclopedia, the metaphoric volume in which I could look up, say, how crows quite specifically communicated, as in "Danger! A man!" or, even more specifically, as in "Great danger! A man with a gun!"

As a father to five myself, I now look back on this with incredulity and horror, but from my ninth year I was set loose as the would-be man with gun; I carried my Remington single-shot .22 rifle, a weapon not much larger than a pistol, wherever I went among those woods and fields.

My father and uncle had one rule, namely that I'd shoot nothing I wouldn't subsequently eat. (The crows were excluded, since they were mistaken to be more harmful than beneficial to the farm.) Rather than shooting less, however, I simply ate more. I became a resourceful camp cook. I knew the flavor of opossum and 'coon, and, more exotically, of blue jay and flicker, that last a tasty morsel of red meat, by the way, rather like a woodcock's, the birds' diets very similar. I have eaten from a haunch of gray fox. I could go on, but another sort of taste prevails.

Though I have remained a hunter, I now greatly regret all that senseless carnage. What I don't regret is a certain awareness that those reckless days engendered. I don't mean—or don't only mean—significant competence with animal habits, with discriminating one tree from another, with how the components of the natural world interact. It's a bit hard to explain what I do mean, but I think it touches on an analogous capacity to track my own mental processes, the interactions of one impression with another, as if they were something outside of myself, like wildlife sign. If so, then those early years did prefigure the rather bookish life I've lived as an adult.

Wallace Stevens once described the modern poem as one of "the mind in the act of finding what will suffice." I agree, though I have my own take on the notion. I'm certain for one thing that this act of discovery is not one that merely happens ad hoc: here is one poem, here is another, here is yet a third, and so on. Discovery as I see it is a lifelong process, one involving, precisely, self-abandonment to many things outside one's person. I want to get at some of those that have, in my case, been weirdly determinative.

I remember well the first real book—not a comic or a childish and short story like something from the Dick and Jane series—that I read at one sitting, or rather one lying. I was in sixth grade, it was wintertime, and I was suffering from a whopping Asian flu. Whenever the fever broke and the symptoms abated, I seemed to have a relapse. I ended up missing almost two full weeks of school. The guilty pleasure of truancy evaporated after a few days, and I grew quite desperate: I couldn't even long for the physical activity on which I usually depended, feeling too weak and sore to contemplate such a thing. And yet I had no other true resources.

My mother was the reading type, at least back then in her thirties. I had willfully resisted her exhortations to take up some damned novel until the day came when I simply felt that staying abed with nothing to do but mope would do me in.

Suspiciously, I eyed the small literary pile Mom had assembled on the lamp-stand. The topmost volume was Pearl S. Buck's *The Good Earth*. I lifted it and began, as much a skeptic as one could be. Then I read and read until I finished the very last sentence, which I did with genuine shock, because I had left my normal milieu, in which at least some version of logic and consecutiveness prevailed. As the cliché has it, I'd gotten lost in a book.

For some reason, whenever I think of that episode, I recall the outsized pickle jar I kept on a shelf at the bed's other side. It contained a headless copperhead snake, preserved in rubbing alcohol. My mother had decapitated the creature with a shovel when I was, I think, in fourth grade, and Lord knows why I displayed it there until I left for college at seventeen. However improbably, the mutilated snake seems the presiding genius, or one anyhow, of this salient memory.

I have not returned to *The Good Earth* since that day (and night), in part for fear that it would seem quaint or plodding, in short, that it would lack the totally transporting effect it had on me back then. But whenever I think of the book, or more accurately of the experience that surrounded my reading of it, I not only see my poor snake in the jar but I also smell that peculiar, cloying odor of fever; I see the umbers and beiges of Pennsylvania's November foliage through the same old window; I feel the rough nap of the embroidered bedspread under which I lie; I taste the Vicks Vapo-Rub which, despite the label's warning, I roll into pea-sized pellets and suck. And all these are somehow interwoven with that near-mystical sense of hovering above the quotidian world, without, uncannily, losing touch with physical properties like the ones just catalogued.

I cannot claim that that maiden experience immediately and forever made me into a dyed-in-the-wool, voracious reader. I was likely in college before I read another whole book at one go, and even then, quite probably, just because I had procrastinated on an assignment in an English course. I may have read a bit more as a teenager (sometimes with scandalous ulterior motives, to impress some girl I particularly yearned for)—I may have read more than I had before the encounter with Ms. Buck's narrative. I know I read and avidly reread Ernest Thompson Seton's *Lives of the Hunted* and *Wild Animals I Have Known,* for example, but I did so story by story, not in one protracted spell.

The all-at-once mode has in fact rarely been mine since, at least with fiction, despite the instance of *A Hundred Years of Solitude,* which I devoured between noon and dawn at my beloved pal Steve Arkin's San Francisco apartment in 1974, and more recently, Dennis Covington's riveting nonfiction account, *Salvation on Sand Mountain,* which took me through a night in a Lubbock, Texas motel.

But I am not really talking about reading habits here. It's something else, however indefinable, and to get a bit closer to it, if ever I can, let me skip from Pearl Buck to my sixteenth year, when, surely quite a bit later than most of its readers, I took up Marjorie Kinnan Rawlings's classic, *The Yearling.* I don't recall a great deal from that book. I vaguely remember the affection I developed for poor, doomed Fodder-Wing, and the awe I felt at Slewfoot the bear, but it's mostly a more billowy impression I summon. It includes a certain bathtub, the upstairs one with claw feet.

I had reached the part in *The Yearling* in which protagonist Jody is forced to kill his beloved pet deer, Flag. When I choose, I can yet feel the hot tears rolling down my face, onto my chest and into the tepid water.

Did I report this development to my bosom friend of those days, Tommy White? I did not. Young men were not enjoined back then to leap into forthright expression of their feelings, as they are now (a development on which I have my own—well, my own mixed feelings). No, I hoarded that state of mind, and I have borne its recollection ever since. The memory has been crucial to me in a variety of ways, is part of what some would call my character, and, chiefly, represents a certain writerly aim on which I have only lately come to something like a grasp.

Further, it instantly blended in mind—as it yet does—with all those associations I had, and still have when I think back on *The Good Earth*. The snake wriggles in with the flu odor; the rough bedspread coexists with the bath water and the scary bear and the savor of Vicks; the dark oak leaves outside my childhood window clap and flutter over the expiring young buck, while diminutive men and women in black pajamas and wide-brimmed hats look up from their field work.

It is all very odd.

When I was about 33, and Frenchified lit theory was becoming all the rage on the tonier college campuses, I found myself in awkward cocktail-party conversation with a colleague, a fellow I liked quite a lot (and still do), who had hopped onto the theoretical bandwagon with both feet. His take on what literature was and what it did seemed at least mildly intriguing, to the degree that I understood it; but I couldn't help thinking that his perspective lacked something essential.

I didn't know at the moment just what the missing ingredient was, and even if I had, I would have stood no chance in disputation with this more learned fellow. I wouldn't stand one today. But on the way home in my car, passing under the canopy of hardwood trees on our dirt road in New Hampshire, it came to me, not as a thought, properly so called, but rather as a sort of sensory cluster: the flu smell again; the dark, shuddering leaves; the huffing final sighs of Flag; the two young peasants conspiratorially smiling at one another over the bent back of their aged Chinese father; tears and warm tub-water; savaged serpent; tangy patent medicine—the sensation, once more, of being at once overwhelmed by all those sensory materials and simultaneously looking down on them. The person designated by the pronoun I was somehow removed from whatever equation this was.

In that exact moment, I now believe, I recognized my terminal inadequacy as theorist or scholar. I couldn't have expressed, even as fuzzily as I seem to do here all these years later, what I felt destined to seek, but I must somehow have surmised, however roughly, that I would seek it in a more lyrical way than my so called training or a conventionally professorial role would enable me to do.

Both as reader and author, it's whatever this complex of associations may represent that I want to recapitulate, something which neither moves me to analysis nor would submit to analysis. It follows no a-b-c through x-y-z agenda. Whenever I've approached that recapitulation, I've felt things to be, again in the words of Stevens (these ones apparently but not really paradoxical), "for a moment, final." I've imagined my mind to have found something that, at least for the fleeting moment, will suffice.

Music

Syd—I Recognize Thy Glory . . .

THOSE WHO KNOW ME, as you do so well, my excellent friend, know also that I've long been deeply in love with what the late Rahsaan Roland Kirk called "Black Classical Music," especially of that era whose great practitioners include Monk, Rollins, Davis, Jackson, Roach, among others. So I'm frequently and unsurprisingly asked about the influence of jazz on my poetry. Whenever the question is posed, I try to avoid any glib answer; but I'm never entirely able. The interplay between the music I cherish and the poems I write is likely beyond words. Indeed, it may be another one of those things that, for a long time, however furtively, I've been trying as a poet to find words for.

That said, one of the surer things I can surmise is that as more or less a formalist, I like feeling the chafe of language against the limits of received (or invented) structure. There is no moral nor even aesthetic stance here: I dislike the formalist/free verse debate, because it too often sounds like a pair of Alpha males in territorial combat, each elevating what he does, which is often all he can do, into virtue, and dismissing what he doesn't and likely can't do as vice. As a rule, the accompanying arguments are downright ill-considered: the free versers, for instance, associate formalism with elitism and political reaction. . . which makes one wonder where the great practitioners of Delta blues and its musical derivatives would stand. Equally vapid arguments—free verse suggests sloppy poetics and fuzzy thinking, say—are too often trotted out on the other side, as if, say, Adrienne Rich were some scatterbrain.

As for me, I like good poetry, be it formalist or vers libre. (Full disclosure: I'm a lot more at ease with free verse than I am with so-called free jazz, but that need not concern us here.) I do what I do not because I regard it as self-evidently superior but because it's what I do, if you'll allow me some circular reasoning. Who knows? My predispositions may be genetic or characterological. I'm no judge of these possibilities.

Robert Frost cannily reminds us that we speak of musical strains, and for me to riff and fill within a form, however self-generated, however unobvious . . . well, that is a pleasure to me, imaginably the grandest pleasure I take from writing. It is a far more significant pleasure, certainly, than any effort at "meaning." I send what I compose into the world without ultimately knowing as much as a reader may discover about "what I am trying to say" (one of my students' favorite locutions).

I think, though, that I do know the how of the saying, and this is where musical influence most likely flows in.

I suspect, in fact, that I'm a poet in some small degree because I'm a failed improvisatory musician. I haven't played for decades, but back when I did, I was just adept enough to know how masterful the real masters are: how they must have lightning reflexes together with long-honed skills; how they must have a vast awareness of prior literature, along with a yen both to honor and to challenge it; how they must cultivate an affection for form even as they marshal the wit and agility to bend form to novel purpose.

Schooled in an obsolescent, humanist way, moreover, and therefore familiar, precisely, with prior literature, I like also to "sample'" my predecessors, a gesture which Hip-Hop may dream it invented, but which has been part of jazz for as long as that mode has existed. Though I'm certain many of my readers miss the effort, I do like to play off favorite writers: Frost himself, Dickinson, Thomas Hardy, at least two of the Romantics, to mention some prominent ones. This sampling—pace Harold Bloom—represents an affection that too many of my students can't feel, because they do not and are not expected to know poetry from any farther back than the Moderns. They may be able to "deconstruct" a Madonna video, say; they may be hip to the musings of Slavol Zizek; but what we used to call the poetic canon is pretty much out of bounds for them. Yet I say this not so much censoriously as compassionately, for they do in fact deprive themselves of a joy.

There's a record (I still sometimes listen to records) featuring Cannonball Adderley and Milt Jackson called *Things Are Getting Better.* If you get the chance, listen to those masters play—and play around with—that old chestnut, "The Sidewalks of New York," of which there are two quite disparate takes on the album. That tune's melody and rinky-dink waltz format are no more sophisticated than those of the jump rope song it oddly resembles, at least to my ear, no more complex than those we encounter in the most perdurable of American forms, the blues itself.

Which makes me free-associate and meditate a bit on one of the literary idols to whom I just referred. In his fragmentary "The Recluse," William Wordsworth wrote as follows:

> . . . Paradise, and groves
> Elysian, Fortunate Fields—like those of old
> Sought in the Atlantic Main—why should they be
> A history only of departed things,
> Or a mere fiction of what never was?

The poet revolutionarily suggested that the old values of epic need not be sought in an epical domain, no longer available in any case; rather, he continued,

> . . . the discerning intellect of Man,
> When wedded to this goodly universe
> In love and holy passion, shall find these
> A simple produce of the common day.

As I have said, it would be hard to imagine a more commonplace composition than "The Sidewalks of New York." And yet notice how Adderley and Jackson, by dint of brain and heart (intellect and holy passion), move inside its frankly banal chord structure without ever losing touch with that structure and its guiding melody. Their improvisations are a wonder and a delight in and of themselves, but the epical dimension, to borrow Wordsworth's term somewhat inexactly, consists in what we could more exactly label flights of the imagination.

Not so long ago in western history, to return to the issue of music and its influence, cultured intellects assumed that such a dimension was accessible only by way of more formally composed music. For the most part, such an assumption preceded the arrival of the Black Classical approach and endured for quite a while after. Indeed, even now, there are those who find such an entrée the only legitimate one. (I suspect, for example, that my brilliant high school music teacher, the late Albert Conkey, may be doing snap rolls in his grave to hear me talk as I do in this reverie.) I don't want to fight with these partisans, that scarcely being the purpose of my attentions here. I began anyhow by expressing my distaste for banal dialectic, and I don't in any event come to these thoughts as champion of jazz over other kinds of composition—except in my own praxis.

The feel of improvisation (rare though scarcely unheard of in highbrow music) is what juices up my forms. Or so I hope. That approach may not work for other poets. But whoever they are, the imaginative flight is what we are all after; these are simply the materials and attitudes that help me get airborne to the small extent I sometimes do.

Yes, as Wallace Stevens, another idol, iterated and repeatedly demonstrated, Imagination is what the poem is all about. The way the great Black Classical composers and musicians manage such a matter is something that has always seemed to me worth trying, and even failing, to emulate in print.

RE: MUSIC

Fleda—Old Time Rock & Roll

I AM VERY MUCH IN LOVE with elegance, trumpets, pomp and circumstance. And Gerard Manly Hopkins, of course: the grandeur, the constraint, the build-up of grandeur by constraint. I love organ pipes and poems that hold the energy of the ages inside their muscular lines.

Which means I used to hope on any given Sunday we'd be singing the hymns in the front section of my old Christian Church hymnal, the section called Adoration and Praise, the ones like "O Worship the King" with music by Haydn: "O Worship the King, all glorious above, /And gratefully sing his wonderful love," and then the sharps—"Our Shield and Defender, the Ancient of days, / Pavilioned in splendor, and girded with praise." Pavillioned. Girded. Good lord, what great words!

And "Joyful, Joyful, We Adore Thee," music from Beethoven's 9th: "Melt the clouds of sin and sadness, / drive the dark of doubt away, / giver of immortal gladness, / fill us with the light of day."

And "Praise to the Lord, the Almighty , the King of creation," that glorious held note on "creation." And "Holy, Holy, Holy," and "Come Thou Fount of Many Blessings." The marriage of simplicity, the 4/4 time, and occasional surprise of language. The joy of return in the rhyme.

I'm sorry to go on like this, but when I get started, I'm singing in my head and can't quit. The hymns, welded to my body, swing into full voice at the first two familiar chords, carrying the weight of centuries, the passion and devotion of centuries.

I'm just saying. The lyrics to contemporary hymns, the ones I've happened to hear, aren't bad, but the music is mundane. The hope, in both hymns and in poetry, is that both will work together. Not that they're separable, of course. Words themselves are music. Like "Pavilioned with splendor." And Hopkins:

> I caught this morning morning's minion, king-
> dom of daylight's dauphin, dapple-dawn-drawn Falcon, in
> his riding
> Of the rolling level underneath him steady air, and striding
> High there, how he rung upon the rein of a wimpling wing
> In his ecstasy! then off, off forth on swing,
> As a skate's heel sweeps smooth on a bow-bend . . . .

Sorry. I overdid it again. I couldn't break off with a line or two. But there's enough here to feel in the lines the press of all his unwritten poems, of his deeply conflicted feelings about the arrogance of writing poems at all as a priest, you can feel his awkwardness, his confusions, his dissatisfactions.

The language is so intense it feels as if the speaker can hardly get the words out. It's a sonnet, but it doesn't read with the smoothness, say, of Shakespeare. The rhythm's rough. The stresses don't land where we'd expect. The words bump against each other, falling and galling and gashing. It's jazz and it's an organ recital in St. Paul's. It's what my own poems look to as their heavenly home. None of this has to do with religion exactly. I'll get to that in a minute.

So, this organ music is playing in the back of my head, and then there's the gray portable record player on the desk in the living room of my childhood. I don't know where we got it—maybe a gift from my grandparents—many things were. It's unlikely my father bought it, since he doesn't spend money if he can help it. There were a small pile of 33s—Beethoven, Bach, Brahms, Sibelius, Dvorak, Grofé, and a few more. He liked to turn them up concert-hall volume. My mother would hold her ears, so he mostly did that when she was gone outside. He could whistle large sections, along with the recordings. These were good, you might say, rich, tense and intense times, his wandering around the house barefoot, whistling, the phonograph full orchestra. I was 12, 13, my body kicking into high gear, the intensity of it all almost too much for our little house on Whitham street.

There were the pile of 33 records I bought really cheap from our ironing lady down the street. I think she'd joined a record club and got an introductory pile of free records, then couldn't keep making the payments. I had so little money, I was glad to have any records of my own. The one I remember had Doris Day singing "Autumn Leaves" in her sweet, breathiness, as if her voice had been airbrushed. I listened to it over and over because it was MY 33.

My mother had several show tune albums—South Pacific, Oklahoma, The King and I are the ones I remember. They were hers, she loved musicals, but we sang along. We knew all the words. We growled our way through "Ole Jud is daid, a candle lights his haid/ He's lookin' oh so peaceful and so nice." And I learned my first French from South Pacific's "Dites-moi /Pourquoi/La vie est belle." When I get started, I can't stop with these, either. I run through the entire song list in my head: "Bali Hai," "Happy Talk," "Some Enchanted Evening," Rosanno Brazzi and Mitzi Gaynor across the room, eyes only on each other. I see my retarded brother Mark hovering over his little red record player singing "Know You, Know You" with "Getting To Know You" from *The King and I*. What it is about those lyrics is that they are so essentially musical, so singable, so aligned with the narrative of the movie that they become embedded in the action and one can't be sung without seeing as well as hearing?

I want there not to be a hair's separation between the dancer and the dance.

In Rock & Roll, too. I became a teenager at the cusp of Rock and Roll. Elvis and Ricky Nelson fought it out in my devotion, but Elvis almost always won. I played and lip synched "Teddy Bear" in my bedroom with my friends. Let this one song stand for the entire stack of my 45s:

> Baby, let me be
> Your lovin' teddy bear
> Put a chain around my neck,
> And lead me anywhere
> Oh let me be
> Your teddy bear.
>
> I don't wanna be a tiger
> Cause tigers play too rough
> I don't wanna be a lion
> Cause lions ain't the kind
> You love enough.
> Just wanna be, your teddy bear
> Put a chain around my neck
> And lead me anywhere
> Oh let me be
> Your teddy bear.

Awful lyrics. Mindless melody. I don't think my generation can claim any sort of superiority to the whiny repetition of contemporary pop songs. Au contraire. But think about it: these lyrics, first of all, played against the male stereotype. Not a lion or a tiger, but a teddy-bear man. On the other hand, Elvis's voice was so sexy, so seductive, it wore the inscape of capture-and-devour within it. Its smooth lines the sprung rhythm of an alternate reading. Is that stretching it? Not much, I'd say. The times they were a changin' and no one realized it yet, but there it was in Elvis's voice, in his body, in his bedroom eyes that were light years from the bedroom eyes of Rock Hudson as he holds Doris Day's perky little face, or even Sinatra, with his citified not-so-much-seduction as cool. Nothing cool about Elvis and nothing cool about the poetry I love. I love poetry that arrives out of the grip of a fully aware emotion. Like Stanley Kunitz's for one example: "Touch Me," and "The Layers," where the feeling and the poem are one thing. I am willfully naïve and/or simple. Not simple as in lazy, I would say.

What about Elvis, then? Surely the lyrics are simplistic, maybe even lazy. But Elvis takes them on like a weight lifter, seeing how high he can get them, clunky though they be. He would rather be singing Gospel. But this is what he's given, what gets him the screams, and so he takes what he knows of gospel, reaches down into the gospel in his soul, and redeems the mindlessness.

There's Ricky Nelson's "Lonesome Town," and "Hello, Mary Lou." Close, but no, the sound is there, the mournful and troubled-youth- eyes are there, but finally, Ricky and I part ways. He has it all right, and that's why we part ways: he's gotten it right. He has practiced until he's gotten it right. Practice is one thing—Elvis worked the same song over so many times his band collapsed before he did—but Elvis and the music were one. He was not a man who made music. He was a man whose existence itself was music that he simply let us in on.

Bobby Darin is closer than Ricky. Patsy Cline. Roy Orbison. Janis Joplin. My list of top 50s and 60s singers is a lot longer than this, but these are the ones that come to mind. I don't know exactly how I know who's true and who's not, and probably I'm wrong about music and wrong about poetry a lot of the time. What I register is the interplay between my heart and the song, and the singer, and the poem and the poet. I hear authenticity when the language itself reaches down into me and twists a knot into—or out of—my being. Not the idea, but the language. Language, I believe, can bypass ideas, can even bypass what we call meaning (which is nothing but ideas), and pierce through to what there are no words for. Call it sex in sexy songs, but what is sex but longing? What are we longing for? Nothing as simple as orgasm. Nothing as simple as being held. The simpler it appears, the more complicated it seems to be.

Whatever it is, below the level of the lyric, the melody, the language of the poem, it's driven to the surface by pressure, by inscape. Take Beethoven: crazy man, drove everyone around him half crazy. Petty, jealous, botched up his relationship with his nephew, fell madly in love with women he really didn't actually want. You can feel the raw scrape of felt life on his skin. You can hear what it is to be human and find that your whole life is driven by a divinity that shapes your end. Driven by the music across whatever obstacles are in the path until you're bruised and bloody, until the music is bruised and bloody.

For most of our history, some of that pressure was built-in: when sex was genuinely dangerous, when every sexual encounter meant possible pregnancy, when getting pregnant meant wrecking your reputation and your life, sexual seduction—whether to give in to it or not—was a matter of life and death. When heaven or hellfire was a real possibility, when every action carried the weight of one or the other for the vast majority of believers, the language of Hopkins, Donne, Milton, carried that tension.

As those fears have abated, it seems as if our emotional palate is muddier, turned to something like angst rather than fear, more global and less personal. The tension hardly knows where to land inside us, how to announce itself, how to play its music in us. The poets, the musicians, who can find it, the ones who find it for me, are the intensely personal ones, who allow angst, even fear, as well as longing and ecstasy, to touch them on their real personal bodies. Who transubstantiate—to use a Hopkinsesque word—rather than translate that felt life. The old time religion, the old time rock & roll, awful as they were in so many aspects, at least held us tightly enough in their grip so that we raised a powerful voice, didn't we?

FOOD

Syd—Wild Black Duck

I AM REDUCING A SAUCE WHOSE recipe came down to me
from my kids' honorary grandmother, Annie Fitch of Grand
Lake Stream, Maine. I hear it bubbling over the stove's low heat;
soon it will look a little like maple syrup, and in due course it will
complement the wild black duck that my wife and I will be sharing
this evening. I mean to grill the bird over oak coals in an outdoor
hearth. I mean, how else would anyone cook it?

I lost my brilliant duck dog Topper twenty years ago, and have
hunted few ducks since. The bitch pup who was meant to be his
successor turned out to have so many major health problems—a
pair of major intestinal surgeries before she was even two—that I
could never train her, and there hasn't been an apt moment since
to find another duck dog, three dogs already in our house quite
enough.

But Topper's death by cancer (a more and more common story
among dogs in our time) coincided with other discouragements.
I used to wait until the second half of our season for the ducks,
the whole month of October given to ruffed grouse over pointing
dogs. But November and December ducks here have always been
the migratory blacks, the red-legged ones come down from Canada,
and as greater and greater chunks of precious wetland have been
lost to so-called development, and as black ducks have increasingly
hybridized with their more adaptable mallard cousins, the species
has been badly threatened. Quite some time ago, then, federal

authorities reduced the limit on black duck to one. That's a worthy measure, but as I say, a discouragement: who wants to rise two hours before dawn, put out his spread of decoys, sit unmoving and so the more bitterly endure a brutal cold, only to take a single shot, retrieve the decoys, his fingers burning with the cold, and paddle back to the truck?

But I jump-shot this one duck, the one we'll enjoy tonight, this past fall in Maine. The weather had been too rainy and miserable for tromping through dense brush for grouse, so my partner Dave Tobey and I floated Tomah Stream in his canoe, the vast majority of ducks too canny to let us drift up on them, but this one lingering just long enough.

My wife and I are mightily craving the evening meal. Not to have eaten wild duck for this much of our long married lives has felt like a deprivation. Not, of course, the sort of deprivation that huge portions of humanity suffer when it comes to nourishment, but one we have registered nonetheless whenever we've spotted a skein of fall blacks in flight overhead or dabbling far ahead of us as we paddle the Connecticut River.

Hunting ducks over decoys is very different from shooting upland birds in New England. Grouse and woodcock inhabit succession forest, the thicker the better, its edges a confoundment of berry-cane, hardhack, popple whip, and so on. Even if one is lucky enough to own a pointing dog who'll pin a ground bird, and I've been multiply so blessed, the instant available to pull the trigger on each of these birds is just that—an instant. One tends to see ducks, on the other hand, well before he can legitimately shoot at them. Often they will circle four or five times before deciding to come into range, and you use your call as expertly as you know how, hoping to draw them right over the floating blocks.

As I write this, then, I picture myself, either alone with Topper or one of his predecessors, or with bosom hunting pals, moving only my eyeballs to keep tabs on the flight. But whether consciously or not—and it's surely a conscious thing now—I likewise take in the austere beauty of late autumn, the dark hues of oak leaves that cling stubbornly to riverside trees, the pilasters of mist rising straight as string from the surface; I smell the wet of Topper's feet and shins; the sun is a pallid disc just breaching Sunday Mountain.

Life is more than worthwhile. A shame it should pass so quickly.

I recall from my childhood how Warner Brothers' cat Sylvester would contemplate Tweetie the canary, his vision morphing into the tiny bird dressed and presented like a turkey, those small frilly leggings on either side, the perfectly browned breast steaming on a platter. I confess to similar hallucinations on spying a duck as it approaches my blind, so greatly do I prefer the taste of wild duck to that of any other wild game. Yes, undeniably, a wild duck on the plate is one of the hunter's great treats. And yet I am certain that my own yen for the bird has something to do with memories that aren't entirely restricted to taste.

My oldest child's namesake, Creston MacArthur, had a tight little cabin on Third Machias Lake. He and I used to spread decoys off a certain point there, and when we were lucky, we might paddle back to the camp with five or six ducks after a morning's hunt. Once the ancient wood-fired cookstove took the chill out of our bones, we'd step outside again to dress the birds, scattering the lovely feathers to the breeze and leaving the insides down in a wetland for mink and 'coon.

Come evening, we'd kindle the outdoor fire in its ring of stones and, having caged the ducks in a basket broiler, we'd lean the handle against a section of cross-laid road grader blade, which Creston had fetched from somewhere, so that the meat stood in front of the fire and would not char.

You didn't want to cook them too long; the juices still needed to run red when you cut into the meat. Creston and I would sit out there in the dark, eating the ducks with our hands as the few loons left on the lake took up their mournful wails. These were old loons, the young ones already flown to open coastal water. Under the stars of late fall, sharp as razors, we heard one another chewing, groaning, sighing with satisfaction. Now and then a fox might bark along the edge of the marsh, or a loitering bittern, who should have been gone with the young-of-the-year loons, would make that thumping sound for which Creston called the bird "post-driver."

Those meals were good. By God, weren't they? So were the old songs he would sing afterwards, his voice at once rough and tuneful, ones passed down by woodsmen and river-drivers: "The Shores of Gaspereau," "The Lumberjack's Alphabet," "Go 'Long Mule," and all the rest. I see Creston lift his chin for the high notes, his eyes near popping, his face the very picture of glee.

I miss him so badly, though he's 37 years in the grave.

I know there was something primitive about our whole ritual. In spite of that (because of that?) there was also something, well, ritual about it too, if you'll spare me the tautology. Even my own family, seeking as we do to buy local meat and produce whenever possible, having insisted when our children still lived at home that we eat together as a family—even my own family has lost some touch with that ritual basis of consuming our foodstuff. We may not resort to McDonald's or one of its odious equivalents; we don't consume prepared or processed food; but we do seem in a hurry: we need to get fuel into our systems like anyone, but professions and projects seem to tug at us.

Our kids are gone from the house, four of the five with their own careers, the youngest almost through college. Robin and I are apt as not on certain evenings merely to scramble a couple of eggs, make a salad, and sit at the kitchen island for a quarter-hour or so before she heads off to prep a law school class and I, in my retirement, having written most of the day if I've been so moved, to find a suitably challenging crossword puzzle, a televised NBA game, a good novel or collection of poems. The notion of a meal as communal, bonding function appears to be fading as quickly as the art of writing letters to post, even in our own rather culturally conservative house.

Tonight's duck will do its part in contravening the anti-ritualism of modern eating habits. My wife is off teaching, and I have spent the better part of two hours getting Annie's sauce just so (though I can't ever get it quite to where she could; I need a little flour to thicken it, as she never did). I will split a passel of oak logs fairly fine, so that they will break down to coals the more quickly (there I go!); I will lay a few strips of paper birch bark into the hearth, arrange adequate kindling on top of it, then tent the hardwood splits over the kindling.

I will remember chill mornings with friends of a lifetime—Landy Bartlett, Joey Olsen, Peter Woerner, Terry Lawson—as we waited for the ducks to give us a peek; I will remember dear dead folks I loved as well: my father, Creston himself. I'll remember the many times around the many twilight blazes.

The people at PETA will never understand something; indeed, in our increasingly virtual world, fewer and fewer people of any persuasion will understand that this ritualism, this recapitulation in a single hunt of all the hunts one has gone on before, especially hunts in dear company, is far more important than a full game bag. The meal that follows, likewise, needs to be ritualized in some way that honors the animate world and the past of that world, in which we mere humans have played our tiny parts.

I think the same might be said of poetry, though I may, again, be among the minuscule portion of modern men and women who will comprehend what I mean by all this.

My history, or at least some glorious moments within it, will burst into mind as the duck's juices burst onto my palate; in fact they have already burst into my thoughts as I write this down. It is perhaps the recollection of wood smoke that slightly burns my eyes until they water a little.

RE: FOOD

Fleda—Fried Chicken and Meatloaf

AH, YOU REMIND ME, your stories remind me, of our revered poet and novelist Jim Harrison's gourmet cooking of the birds and animals he shoots, or used to shoot, himself. A poetry fed by variety and by a raw and intimate relationship with other living things. I don't think I tasted duck until I was forty. No one I knew was a hunter. Could you buy duck in the grocery store, then? I don't know. If it was exotic, we wouldn't have had it. My mother wasn't much of a cook. My father liked his food perfectly plain, and when she went to any trouble with a new preparation or sauce, he would say, "I don't know why you wanted to do that. . . ." And her mother—we lived next door to her for several years— was a good cook and also had a maid who cooked. Furthermore, her mother-in-law loved to cook and tore hundreds of recipes out of magazines, stashing them between the pages of already well-worn cookbooks. My terribly insecure mother would throw hunks of pot roast beef in the new-fangled pressure cooker until they were pale and stringy. She would fry liver to leather, and produce slabs of round steak that required zealous chewing. We had frozen peas, frozen mixed vegetables, plain as God made them.

Sometimes my father would get a bug for cooking, always in an effort to save money. He bought cow's tongue because it was cheap, and, not knowing what else to do with it or caring about anything other than getting it cooked, he threw it in the pressure cooker. The result was a rough, slightly curled tongue lying on the plate looking as if it had just been severed from the cow's mouth. My sister and I were each required to eat a chunk. It tasted like cardboard, but it was the little bumps on the surface that made me gag. Another time he cooked the boysenberries he picked from the bushes out front. Jam, I guess it was, a little thick and not enough sugar, as I remember. He would fly into a rage if we complained that something didn't "look good." The idea was to eat it, not look at it.

✧

I'm not fair to my mother. She made great fried chicken, mashed potatoes, and meat loaf. She whipped the potatoes with the Sunbeam mixer and put tons of butter and salt on them. She ground together beef and sausage to make very good meatloaf, using the hand-cranked grinder we still have in the basement. As did apparently everyone else in the 50s, she mixed various kinds of canned fruit into Jello and called it salad—although we did have real salads. She loved to make cakes and occasional pies. Sometimes I'd come home from school and there'd be a grand cake, all frosted, and she'd be a proud as a kid. You get the idea: plain food. But always decent food and always on the table, served on indestructible Melmac dishes, at dinner time.

Indestructible dishes because first of all, my mother dropped and broke every dish or glass that would break. Second, my retarded brother would wave his hands around, hitting dishes, and his grand mal seizures could come at any time. We ate on Melmac, we drank out of aluminum tumblers. (Plastic was in its infancy then). And there was an indestructable "dinette set," table and chairs with metal legs slanted space-age-y outward, the table-top a vinyl fake wood grain. Meals were okay, sometimes tense if my father had money on his mind, or if we were waiting for my brother to recover from a seizure. Or sad, if my father had been yelling and my mother fighting back tears. When I think of food from those days, I think of staring at the table, not up into the room or into people's faces. Just eating, liking the food okay, concentrating on the food. We didn't look into each other's faces. I just now realized this. Which makes me think of Wilder's "Our Town," of Emily's recognition that her family didn't see each other when they were all together; they weren't aware of their lives. It seems to take a return, it seems to take recollection, to really see. And of course this is the writer's mind, that keeps returning, wanting not just to see it in the mind but to get it down, feel its texture, see what to make of it at last.

So I see it now. We were all there. About the food, I have no reason to complain. At a time when most were eating Wonder Bread, we ate Roman Meal. Mostly because my father came from a family that highly valued nutrition, we didn't eat things that were bad for us. Very few Cokes or candy bars, no potato chips except for very special occasions. "Junk," he called it, and I knew, and know, it was and is.

When we traveled to the cottage in Michigan, or to my grandparents' house in Missouri—the only trips we made—my mother packed the Thermos lunch kit. There were two tin compartments for sandwiches, usually peanut butter and jelly, plus sometimes fried chicken. There were two Thermos bottles, one for milk, one for water. There might have been packets of cut-up carrots. No "prepared" food. I can smell the brown fake-leather case as she unzipped it for lunch, the metallic odor of the food boxes, the faint chicken smell, and the cool, slightly unusual taste of milk stored for hours in a glass thermos.

At that time, there was very little prepared food, anyway. As TVs became ubiquitous, there were TV dinners. But no one had yet figured that a lot of money could be made by packaging food in small portable portions, adding lots of sugar and salt, and making preparation a snap. There were no microwaves.

There was no "ethnic" food in Northwest Arkansas, to my knowledge, until I was in college, when the Venetian Inn opened in nearby Tontitown and became all the rage: slabs of beef and a lettuce salad with a perfect vinegar and oil dressing that we later found out was laced with beer. And then Suzy Wong's in a little house a few miles out of town. "Suzy" and her policeman husband had been to China. They served plum sauce that she smilingly said came from plum trees on the property. Several years later, she admitted that there were no plums in the plum sauce, just sugar, food coloring, and a bit of rice wine vinegar.

↝

I do like a good dinner, a beautifully presented one. I'm a good cook when I try hard, but the skill isn't built into me. The first stage of my planning a dinner party is panic: "Oh Lord, I've gotten myself into it again!" The second stage is digging through cookbooks, getting interested. The third dreaded stage is the shopping. The final one I enjoy: the actual cooking. And the actual evening with friends.

So, what was it like for my children? Breakfast was our best meal, when my second husband, their step-father, was still asleep and couldn't dominate the room. I'd alternate between oatmeal, Ralston, sometimes with pancakes, and on Sundays we'd make cinnamon rolls out of a can, the kind that comes with a small container of icing to dribble over the rolls. A huge treat. What I remember is just the peace, the nice little time together at the picnic table in the kitchen.

As for dinner, I was famous for hitting 6:00 on the dot. Dinner's ready. I went through spurts, as I do now, of cooking from recipes, but much of the time it would be the trifecta: something brown, something white, something green, as my children liked to say. I am pretty good at adding, playing around with preparation so what goes on the table is better than ordinary. For example, last night I took baby portabella mushrooms and onions and stir fried them a bit, added chicken breasts, soy sauce, and a little white wine. Very brown and pretty on the plate next to sautéed red pepper and garlic. Plus always a huge salad.

Food as the dark, rich taste of the past, bursting on my tongue? It's more double-edged for me: a combination of love and dread, the gathering at the table itself an opportunity both for warmth and for misery. Food prepared because it must be, not because it will be raved over, or the effort appreciated. But it is appreciated. Now I appreciate it. Did I say that then? What did I say when I pushed my metal chair back from the table? Did I say "Thank you for this food, for this life?" I'll say it now.

Sex

Syd—Pony and Graveyard: A Dream of the Flesh

A TRICKY ONE FOR ME, this subject. Its once-upon-a-time must start at ten years old or so, before I understood sexuality except by some vague surmise, In those days, I habitually rode Warrior Maiden, my fat little Shetland pony, past Angie Morton's house. Angie was sixteen, I think, and movie star beautiful, at least in my eyes. She was scarcely taller than I, and would never grow taller, but her figure was simply statuesque. She had raven hair, almost chalk-white skin, and the most penetrating eyes, ice-blue, almost white themselves, I had ever seen or would ever see after.

My hope, often enough repaid, was to catch her in her yard or, far more exciting, for reasons I must also have dimly surmised, through her bedroom window. No, that's not accurate: the compensation for my hope was never adequate. True, I couldn't conceive what satisfaction might entail, but I knew Angie's languid wave or, on happier occasions, her desultory word or two of chitchat was not it.

So desperate was my need for this young woman, whatever the need comprised, that I frequently extended my rides just so I could pass her house more than a single time on a single ride. I remember tethering Warrior Maiden to an apple tree and simply sitting under it for as long as I could bear, gorging on the wormy windfalls till I made myself queasy. At least I thought the fruit was to blame for how I felt.

These delaying maneuvers resulted once in a frightening but thrilling trip home after dark. In our corner of Montgomery County lay a small settlement of southern-born blacks, who had made the hard trek north in search of better fortunes. Most of them went to work in an asbestos mill in Ambler, though a fair share took jobs on local farms, or, if they were women, they labored as domestics in the more prosperous households. I found their little dwellings fascinating and somehow foreboding: in the warmer months, the front doors seemed always open, but the interiors were kept so dark that I could never quite make out the figures inside. In one tiny house, a harmonica seemed always to be playing, though I couldn't find the musician. Each shack seemed multi-generational: I could tell that much by the wide variety of human heights among the shadowy occupants.

The shantytown had an aroma of cuisine, exotic, at least to me, pungent, and attractive; but the truly unusual feature of the community was its cemetery, with those knife-thin, tilting headstones, each adorned and surrounded by shards of broken glass, and the bordering trees full of suspended bottles. To ride by that half-acre graveyard plot after sunset, and after having laid my adoring eyes on Angie; to hear indistinct rustlings of nocturnal animals in the brush; to be forced to rely solely on the pony's sense of where home lay: this mixture of adventure, reverence, mystery, fear and trespass would come to serve as a kind of under-aura to such sexual experiences as I would have in my adolescent years— and later ones too.

However strangely it strikes me today, I seem somehow to have believed that my life would never amount to anything, that I would never know that obscure condition people called happiness, if I couldn't be with Angie, even if, as I've conceded, I didn't understand what that sort of "being with" entailed.

The notion was absurd, of course, and yet it didn't end as I came to maturity, at least of the physical kind. For too many years, I would spot a woman in some public place—museum, train, airport, restaurant, campus—and would be convinced that if I could not know her in the Biblical sense my entire life would be no better than despair. The inane measures I took to guarantee myself, if not a conversation with her, at least a glimpse of my exalted Angie were paltry compared to the extraordinary lengths I went to in order to put my person in the way of these coveted women. I can't even describe the sanest of those tactics, so embarrassed do I remain by reflection on them.

The tactics, of course, were almost always met with rebuff, or simple non-recognition. Indeed, such a response was no more than I expected, the expectation itself a carry-over from my horseback days. Not that Angie ever cruelly rejected me. I suspect she knew full well the profundity of my crush on her, but she spared me all mockery, let alone recourse to nasty words. She appeared always to have enough time for a brief exchange of remarks, which I both craved and resented.

None of her acknowledgments was enough. However banal my part in the conversation, I always hoped she could read it allegorically somehow, could know that my commentary on the weather, for example, was freighted with double-entendre. Alas, she never appeared to decode the allegory, and despite my knowing, even at ten, that her failure to do so owed itself to my own clumsiness and to no defect in her, I was free to regard the failure as a kind of dismissal. Unrequitedness thus became, as I say, an expectation.

I will be forgiven for lacking the temerity as a child to declare my devotion to the paragon Angie. But that I should remain oblique, even prudish to this day when it comes to talking about sex seems an odd thing, so elaborate and ardent were my efforts as a young man to get as much of sex as permitted by such charm as I owned and by 1950s mores, which I felt both thrill and shame to violate when I could. Before I was able to publish the one and only novel I ever composed, for example, my agent had practically to horsewhip me into juicing up my characters' erotic encounters. Though the first draft referred to those encounters, it stopped leagues short of depicting them. In forty years of teaching, for further instance, I never felt other than acutely uncomfortable when discussing student work that showed significant carnal content.

One problem that has always concerned me, at least in my avatar as prose essayist, is what I call the temptation to closure. That is, I may lay out a series of memories, emotions, and events, and then discover myself hunting for a way to herd them into a narrative corral. I don't know if that's what I am doing here. I honestly do not. In any case, I wonder if my unease in talking about sex out loud or on the page may go back to a certain horseback ride after dark, when—full of vague lust, longing, and melancholy—I passed what was then referred to as the Colored Graveyard. The sense, as I lingered under Angie Morton's window, that I was on the brink of an exciting but forbidden trespass may have been further impressed on body and soul by my traveling on horseback by those darkened cabins, each so full of mystery, then under those suspended bottles, which seemed to betoken a universe I had no right to visit. That, after all, was what made it so scintillating to imagine.

RE: SEX

Fleda—The Secret Dark

OH YES, ON THE BRINK, where everything feels utterly alive. No wonder I remember those days so clearly. We would sneak out in the dark with our cans of beer to his parents' car behind his house. They were all home, thinking we were in his room listening to records. We "made out" and drank beer, the windows steamed up so much that we were encased in our own breathing. I was what, fifteen?

It was the secret dark, it was the strangeness. Or we would park. Some road I can't remember, only the rutty feel of it, the dark, "Unchained Melody" on the radio. What did we do there? We kissed with our lips and our tongues, we touched, we trembled. The trembling was because of the strangeness, and because of the opposites that were held so opposite the thought of their union was like the "twin halves of one august event" in Hardy's poem "The Convergence of the Twain," where "the Spinner of the Years / Said "Now!" And each one hears, / And consummation comes, and jars two hemispheres."

I'm not saying it was like that, I'm saying this is what our minds did with it, the huge event that was huge, then, really. This was before 1960 when the pill was approved for contraceptive use. Sex mattered.

Besides that, sex was an adventure. We didn't have soft porn spread over billboards and on nightly TV and easily found on the internet.

We didn't have movies with sex so blatant and casual that it seems more like taking a shower or working out at the gym. It was rich with mystery, it felt religious, breathlessly close to God.

What was the course of my own sexual adventure? There was Jay MacDonald. I had loved him from afar in the sixth grade. I had asked him to join my stamp club. Yes, stamp club! We met two or three times in my basement. Did he come? I can't remember. Then when I got to Junior High, I asked Bob Thurlby to the Sadie Hawkins Day sock hop. His parents brought him to pick me up. He was clearly given instructions to meet my parents. There was my father, sprawled out on the living room floor trying to repair our old Zenith console radio, our house a wreck. I whisked us out the door as fast as possible. Bob, a perfect gentleman, must have danced with me the first and the last dance. All I really remember is the awfulness of sitting with the girls on the bleachers. I was not popular. I was not unpopular. I was, or thought I was, invisible.

⌖

It may be invisibility, or the perception of it, that helps make a writer. I was watching, feeling unwatched. I was storing up, registering. Suffering my teenage angst, but suffering it as if I were a bit schizoid, watching myself suffer.

Let us just look, briefly, later, in the window of the 1958 Buick Skylark. Let us watch the young couple there, side by side, barely touching in the dark. It's clear that something has happened, something to make them move apart in a gesture of renunciation. He's swearing that this will never happen again. She's sniffling. They are so in love with love that the movement apart seems like a grand dance, a fluid turn and stop, the radio going on with its urging. Nothing is better than this.

Sex was the container, not the rules. The rules—whether adhered to or not—were that you didn't do this until marriage. The rules implied that the act of touching each other in secret places had to do with touching each other's secret emotional places. That such touching involved commitment—a merry-go-round of logic that came down to Doris Day's popular song, "Love and Marriage, love and marriage / go together like a horse and carriage."

Sex itself, though, under legal conditions, was not at all rule-bound. It came, and comes, from the emotional core, the need that has no words and no schedule. "It"—meaning the moves, the speechless drive—contained everything wanted, everything hoped for. It really, truly was religious. It was our heavenly home. Those who giggled, those who made lewd jokes, those who drew anatomical pictures on the inside wall of the bathroom stalls—they were only affirming the power of what they mocked.

I was too young to understand such depth of longing but—for many reasons irrelevant here—my emotional needs were huge. The second year of church camp, I fell in love with Bo Parker. We were camp "King" and "Queen" for one day, crowned at breakfast with paper crowns. The camp's evening ritual was for everyone to gather at the dining room door after dark and sing "Jacob's Ladder" or some such as we wound together down the hill to the spillway rocks for a bonfire, guitars, and more singing. Bo and I were sitting together a little apart from the others, the fire casting a radiance on the flat expanse of rock, the spillway far below us in the dark. He slipped his hand around my back, gently, barely touching. I leaned in toward him. Did we kiss? I can't be sure now. What I do remember is the feeling of religious devotion and love: inseparably, breathlessly intertwined.

In 1958, probably the very same year, there was a movie, *Sing Boy, Sing*, in which Tommy Sands played an Elvis-like young singer who becomes a star. I have a faint memory of a scene where he goes to visit his preacher father, maybe it was, and ends up on his knees, praying. I remember nothing else except that the combination of God and sex left me panting with desire.

The next day Bo Parker avoided me entirely. Somehow I got a message—through someone—from him, that he didn't "want to get serious." In truth, I saw quickly that he had a crush on a blonde counselor. I lay in my bunk, utterly crushed, reading my Bible for consolation, a last resort. I understand the lyrics of love songs in which the lover feels he can no longer live without his love.

My heart went everywhere, anywhere there seemed to be an opening. I would have kissed a toad. I have kissed a few. I got married when I was seventeen, which probably saved me from a worse fate. All this I've written about elsewhere. Well, not all. Some things are meant to be kept forever private.

Which is where I started with this. Privacy makes for excitement, for passion. In writing and in life. Withholding makes for awareness. What I mean by this is that when we don't have something, or deny ourselves something, or when something has been denied to us, the outlines of it come clear. White space matters.

And when we have everything, when we have years of a good marriage, when the skin begins to get crepy and fallen, when the heart is willing and the flesh is weak, when a good book and a bright fire are about as fiery as the flesh feels some days. No one talks much about that, as if it's a sad shame. Though it's not. There's no stage of the body's progress that seems like a shame.

To get to this, this moment in bed together with our books and thick blankets seems like a triumph of the human spirit, and is, to my mind. What was it I wanted, all those years ago, but to be held gently by the universe? Oh, wait. I wanted riotous sex, desperate, panting sex.

What is, what was that all about, that desire beyond imagining, beyond hormones? That unquenchable longing to merge, to be swallowed up in something or someone else? To be inside a story I didn't write. To be found there. It was a false hope, it turns out. To be found, I only had to inhabit my own self, my own voice, my own story, fully. This took years. And what have I found: this body in its inextricable fragility. The passionate world collapsing gloriously around me.

Houses

Syd—Wistful: The Yellow House

A T $35,000 IT DID SEEM A BIT PRICEY for the neighborhood. On the other hand, I was making all of $9600 a year, plenty to service the $108 monthly mortgage debt, and the house was so perfectly located, my wife and I agreed, that we'd be foolish not to snap it up.

As in fact we did. It was a nineteenth-century farmhouse at the foot of Kenyon Hill, right across the dirt road from Fred Wagner's fire pond and backed up against mile upon mile of untouched woodland. Any kids we might have would be safe from cars and trucks, there was ample room for a truck garden, and as for me, I could hike and hunt as much as I wanted. All I needed to do was to walk out the mudroom door and climb a few hundred yards.

We moved in that April of 1968, the prior winter's back broken, and no sons or daughters yet to keep out of the considerable mud that lay all around us, as we learned to do later. More than once, that mud bogged my trail-worn Ford Fairlane up to its hubs, but I rarely had to call a wrecker; some kind neighbor would pass the house in his big farm truck or tractor and yank me out.

For my part, I felt I had gone to heaven. Oh, there were a few problems with the antique boiler, but with help from the late, generous Don Welch of Bradford Oil, I learned how to tweak it just so and get it up and running again—most of the time. Don also taught me how to fiddle with the air volume control on the equally ancient water pump, so as to make it kick in again too. I was not only undismayed by these little chores; I rather savored them as part of life in the north country.

Come May, I set about cutting enough wood—or so I thought—to get us through the winter. I was young and strong, and there was ample timber to be had from a neighbor's lot that he wanted thinned. So I decided to be more than safe, even to get a little ahead for the second winter we'd live there, so I cut and split and stacked ten full cord.

I might save time and breath here by simply saying that ten cord was not sufficient to keep our stoves blazing through the first winter. The stove in the living room was a Round Oak, and it was gorgeous, all filigree and finial, with actual mica in the door, through which a cozy gleam seeped into the living room. But the thing was as archaic as everything else in the building, loose and leaky, its firebox mere sheet metal, which at times—even with the draft closed as tight as it would go—glowed so red that I dared not turn my back on it, for fear the whole thing might simply melt away and burn the house to the ground.

One weekend night, tired from hunting birds all day, I grew impatient. Unwilling to wait until the fire cooled a bit, and the stove stopped showing that alarming scarlet, I shoveled some sand in to put the damned blaze out. I hadn't imagined there'd be enough remnant moisture in that sand for a steam explosion to blow the isinglass right out of the door, and that I'd be stamping live coals on the wide spruce boards of our floor. The charring would still be there when at long last the marriage collapsed and we sold the house.

I likewise remember a certain spot under the kitchen counter, which simply could not be adequately heated to prevent the sink's pipes from bursting whenever the mercury dropped to twenty below or lower. I tried my amateur hand at all manner of insulation. I even wrapped the pipes with electrical heating tape; but in time I read of one too many houses that had been incinerated by malfunction of such a device. I hired local contractor Wayne Pike to work on the problem, but highly competent as he was, none of his measures worked either.

We had another stove in the kitchen, but there was no cellar under that room, the result being that one could feel warm as toast there—except from about mid-shin down. So cold did it get along that floor, with its fake-brick linoleum cover, that whenever the pipes did burst, the water would turn to instant, crackling ice beneath our feet.

I was attentive to local weather forecasts, and when they predicted cold snaps of that sort, I would drain the pipe and shut it off, by reaching my hand as far and as painfully as I could into the small space between earth and boards and turning a valve handle. But even then, there would often linger enough water that the copper would burst. I must have sweated thirty new joints in that pipe over the course of fifteen years.

My older son is now forty-one. He arrived in 1971, and in his second year he took to peeling the plaster on his bedroom wall. At length he created a head-sized hole there. To look into the hole was to discover what the house had for insulation: corncobs, old newspapers (one of which headlined the sinking of the *Lusitania*), and here and there a bit of sawdust, though that was likely the product of rodents, who trod within those walls so freely that among other things they tamped all this ancient insulation down to about knee level.

Cold wind, especially from the northwest, would send small gales through electrical sockets and nail-holes all through the house. And although I cut as much wood every year as many a lumberjack did in his trade, or so it felt, we always wanted to wear our felt-lined Sorel boots indoors, along with at least a wool vest, sometimes a parka.

As I say, the marriage guttered, mostly thanks to my own ill behavior, but not until after the arrival of yet another child, a wondrous daughter. Both these children are parents now, and they are so good at that crucial role that I sometimes blink in astonishment.

I moved into a new house, married another extraordinary woman, and three more children arrived. Then we moved once more, again to a new house. Like any, it has its own occasional problems, but in the thirty-odd years since abandoning the yellow one, I have encountered nothing on the scale presented by that old firetrap.

This house—the last, I pray, that I'll inhabit—sits on a piece of land even more beckoning than that first plot: from a small knoll behind us, we can survey at least five miles of the Connecticut River, farm fields and barns spread along it, and, on a clear day, we can see deep into the White Mountains on the New Hampshire side. Rather than a tiny fire pond, we have a seven-acre one that attracts all sorts of waterfowl, otters, mink, muskrats, deer, moose.

It seems strange, then, that I am occasionally wistful for that rickety first house, with its rat-trodden insulation and boreal indoor winds, with its damnable bursting pipe, its cranky boiler and pump. I still cut wood for our heater stove, but now four cord will do for a winter, and sometimes less, the weather rarely turning as frigid as it did when I was in my twenties and thirties. The roof is of standing seam metal, so I needn't climb on top to shovel off the snow, an enterprise so burdensome and risky at once that I'm glad to have it well behind me, though to be sure, the snow doesn't pile up the way it used to, either.

Early on in this collaboration, Fleda asked,

> Don't we all start in on elegy—writers or not—at about age 13, when the gap begins to reveal itself to us, the sense of having an irretrievable past—our childhood—as well as a present, which holds what's already coming into being?

Yes, of course. Of course it's not really the house that I'm nostalgic about. It's a season of life, especially right at the start, when I felt up to anything, when everything struck me as so sharp, so new, and when those older children—long since grown and gone—were no more than dreams of the future.

RE: HOUSES

Fleda—I Am In Love with Houses

I'VE BEEN IN LOVE WITH HOUSES, too, even those I hated, which of course were the ones with all the possibilities. My patient husband tells me I decorate a house as if I were writing a poem—with that kind of exactitude and infinite revision.

My grandparents lived next door to each other on South Garth Avenue in Columbia, Missouri—a settled and tree-lined neighborhood. One set of grandparents lived in House Beautiful (405 S. Garth) and the other in a beautiful house (403 S. Garth): both craftsman-style with front porches and glassed-in "sleeping porches" above. Both with glorious secret places. The Browns' house had beveled glass windows in the dining room. The stairs rose gracefully up two landings. The Simpiches' house featured dark wood pillars separating the entryway from the living room. Each house had a fireplace and a sliding pocket door to the dining room.

When my family moved to Arkansas and we lived that year in barracks-style student housing, it felt like camping out. I was eleven, and didn't care, for a while. I liked the mud holes, the kids running loose through the neighborhood, and the furniture my parents ordered unassembled from Sears and my father put together. It was an adventure. After that was the tiny rental house just off campus and across the street from Mr. Mack's tiny grocery, and then the flat subdivision house my parents bought on Maxwell Drive. Houses plucked down in a semicircle in a field, each a small variation on the next. Nothing to imagine, no way, it seemed, to make them sing. Or dance. Hence, I guess, my longing.

Longing for what? Not exactly for the mythical houses of my grandparents, the ones elevated in memory. Maybe for beauty itself. I've been passionate about every house I've lived in, even the one on Maxwell Drive, where I singlehandedly pruned the mass of irises along the driveway. I must have been fourteen. I think it was that same year, I had a friend whose name is now lost to me, who invited me to her house for the afternoon. Her family had rented a sad corner house not far from our school. I had the feeling that they moved often. Her room had almost nothing in it but a bed and a turned-sideways wooden milk-crate thing for her dresser. Her clothes were few and worn. I remember her room because it had nothing in it. It echoed. But there was that milk crate with a cloth on it and a few bottles on top and one necklace of blue beads. I thought how cute the crate was with its things arranged on it, how I would like to do that for myself. What I was feeling, as I think of it now, was that longing I mentioned, my need to gather, to see beauty or the reaching for beauty anywhere it could be found. I suddenly think of the end of Elizabeth Bishop's poem, "Filling Station:"

> Somebody embroidered the doily.
> Somebody waters the plant,
> or oils it, maybe. Somebody
> arranges the rows of cans
> so that they softly say:
> ESSO—SO—SO—
> to high-strung automobiles.
> Somebody loves us all.

❧

Then there's Keats: "Beauty is truth, truth beauty." At fourteen, what possible connection could there be between artfully arranging my own things on my dresser and truth? The only truth I knew anything about was the not-telling-lies kind. But I was working this out, the connection, in houses:

When I was very young, the Browns' house seemed less glamorous than the Simpiches'. The Browns' house had bare wood floors, nubby greenish-brown sofa and chair, a record player in the living room, and a big old-fashioned enamel sink in the kitchen. I don't know how to describe that house exactly except that it felt used and worn and essential. There was a sparseness I didn't know how to identify, which, as I studied each set of grandparents, came to mean something about the life I wanted for myself. I couldn't have said that then.

The Simpiches had wall-to-wall carpeting. They had one of the first console TVs and one of the first air conditioners. Their house was my dream house. Every few years, they got new furniture and had the downstairs re-carpeted. At Christmas, the trees changed with the fashion—it was glorious to arrive, all of us scruffy and worn from the day-long drive from Arkansas, and find a white flocked tree with all pink round lights on it. And then another year an aluminum tree with miniature lights. Other years a full, beautiful evergreen with bubble-lights. In the summer, Nana would be in her garden in the early morning picking roses, zinnias, sweet peas, and lilies. Her large garden had vegetables, fruit, and flowers, and then when you walked out through the arbor, there was the fishpond (with my handprint in the cement), and on the other side of the walk, a sitting area with Adirondack chairs. Perfectly beautiful, all of it.

The Browns' back yard had a walnut tree that made us all rich with nuts in the fall, and it had a swing on the catalpa tree, and a scrawny crabapple tree. On the north side were lilies of the valley. It was a yard to use without thinking much about it, to get crabapples and walnuts from and to swing in. When my family lived for a while in the Browns' house, I would go back and forth, yard to yard, part of my mind assessing and measuring something. I am sure I was doing that, because I began to imagine my life, very early, as a matter of either/or. My parents were both still children, never having broken the child's primal attachment to their parents-as-supreme authority. I guess it was natural for me to look to their parents, also, to figure out how to be in the world.

There was something at Nana's house that I felt in my bones, a careful arranging of objects that was meant—what shall I say?—to hold things down, to demonstrate. Not an "act" exactly, but somehow a secondary layer. I don't have words for this, really. At the Browns', there was a strangeness—prunes for lunch and conversations about the economy that I didn't understand—but even though I was working on rejecting that world for not being pretty enough, I was taking it in and finding it authentic in some way the other wasn't.

I myself have been the most dedicated of arrangers, of furniture choosers, of house beautifiers. I love beauty around me. Jerry and I have spent money on art, for sure. We have better taste than the Simpiches, I guess you could say, but that isn't really the point. The point is, what beauty? What truth?

I am, like my grandfather Brown, an academic. And, like several of my ancestors—some published a bit, some not—a poet. Like my grandfather Brown, my delight is words and ideas. I feel a deep kinship with him. But I also feel a deep kinship with my Nana Simpich, who seemed to me to be unsure. To be nervous in her effort to get things right and to demonstrate that she'd indeed done that. Aren't we all unsure as well as sure? Don't we all know as well as don't-know? This describes me, I have to say. Both of these are the truth.

↜

I see that I've kept from you the deepest rudder of my taste, the principle, or I should say the longing that has informed my every shifting of furniture, every painting of a wall, every choice of blinds or curtains. It is the old family cottage at Central Lake. I guess I've kept this information back because it's so dear that I hold it privately to my heart. It's bigger than aesthetics—it is a principle that I am suddenly aware connects me with the Browns' house in Columbia: the cottage and everything in it exists to be used. The layer I might call adornment is stripped away. It is to sleep in, to fish from, to swim away from, to cook in and eat in. Its form is its function.

I think for form to be function—in writing as well as in living—form has to have a great deal of confidence in itself as essential expression. It must get free of a great deal of its self-consciousness. It must not doll itself up too much. It must not be bigger, more elaborate, than necessary. It must hold people to each other. The spaces must accommodate but not exaggerate. They must not be McMansions.

The Browns, from what I know, were messy. No one cared if there was an old galvanized tub sitting in the yard all summer for no reason, or an outboard motor clamped to a board between two trees in the front yard. No one cared if there were several children "sunbathing" on the cottage roof. There were my father, my uncle, my aunt, their grandmother and sometimes their other grandfather staying with them in the summer. Somehow they all fit. Part of the porch was walled in to make another bedroom. Another part was screened in to make an eating porch.

As I said, I have mythologized all this. It doesn't matter. The past is always a mixture of fact and fantasy. The past with the musty, cedary smell of the cottage just opened for the season, the fireplace smell, the lake smell even with its faint gasoline fumes, the lapping of lake water on the stones: that past is real. And because the cottage now belongs to me and my sister, it exists in the present as well.

For many years, through two marriages, I lived in houses that gave me very little, no matter how hard I tried to shape them. I felt that I had no choice in the matter. You can see that I'm not just thinking about houses, but how they come to stand for our lives, in toto. The houses of my own life have grown more beautiful. Twenty-one years ago I married my dear Jerry. Our first house together was on the Elk River just where it flows into the Chesapeake Bay. At last a house that approximated the feel of the Michigan cottage. You could actually see the Bay through the trees in winter, and there was a path down to a community beach. Then after we decided the drive to our teaching jobs at the University of Delaware was too great a distance, much closer to town we bought a Lindal cedar house—one built from a kit—on two acres of woods with a small stream in back. Water and trees. The essentials. We both choked up when we left it to move to Michigan.

But we retired, sold that house, gave half our furniture to our children, and moved an hour's drive from the cottage, into a small old house—Craftsman-style, like my grandparents' houses—in an old neighborhood with lovely cracked sidewalks. I think when I first caught sight of the cracked sidewalks, I fell in love, and I can tell you exactly with what —it was what I at least perceived as a kind of truth, the truth of people being neighbors, of biking and walking their dogs and pushing their strollers, of rubbing shoulders with each other, of living close enough together, in small enough houses, to do that. People seeing each other as they are, reaching for the newspaper in their bathrobes. This may be another fantasy of mine, but it feels right to me, this life where people are immediate, present, and unavoidable. This life feels essential.

I've loved this house—we've painted, repaired, built two new dormers. It looks good. And if you walk out the front door, turn left, and stand in the middle of the intersection, you can see Grand Traverse Bay five blocks away. Knowing the water is there is enough. We only have two trees, but there's the cottage waiting for us. Waiting for summer.

Illness

Syd—To Take a Flop

I CAN'T COUNT THE WAYS IN WHICH my life has been blessed.
Wife. Children. Grandchildren. Friends. Those would be the
primary gifts I'd catalog, but if I sat and thought about my past
and, even more, my present, there'd be innumerable others. I could
muse at length, say, on the score of dogs we have owned, their
eccentricities at home and, in the case of the working ones, afield.
I could muse at equal length on the miracles ensuing from the
decision to make my way as a poet: the people I've met; the students
I've loved; the places to which I've been invited.

But another fabulous blessing is one I tend to forget until it is
suspended. I mean my health. It has been significantly interrupted
only twice in 69 years, once by something life-threatening, a second
by something that menaced my soul.

On Labor Day, 1994, I was one of several local neighbors who set
out to do some local good. A village woman's husband, who proved
even more a narcissist than we had surmised, which is to say a
mouthful, had abandoned her and their two small children in the
dead of night, having not only raided their joint bank account but
furtively, little by little, their woodshed.

We decided to cut our neighbor a big pile of hardwood, using
the well-dried tops of trees, remnants of the past winter's timber
harvest on the land my wife and I own.

I was more than willing to join this posse, but I was also eager to get back home to our own small kids, who after all had this bonus day off from school. And so, despite having wielded a chain saw for hundreds and hundreds of hours in my life, I grew careless. I was "bullin' and jammin'," as an old Vermonter would put it, and dressed in sneakers, socks and a pair of running shorts, period. Just the week before, I had put off buying the Kevlar chaps without which I don't even start the saw since.

I'd seen the chaps at *Deb's Wheel and Deal* across the river. Deb, an attractive woman who was small but tough as nails, able to face down the meanest roughneck logger who sassed her in her store, had them on sale for eighty dollars. I'd long since finished cutting my own supply of wood for the coming cold months, and told Deb that eighty felt a bit rich for my blood at the time. She smiled wryly, and as it turned out, prophetically: "A lot cheaper than the emergency room," she said.

At one point, rather than stepping right up to it and planting my feet, I reached to cut a limb off a felled oak, and just as I did, stepped into a hole. Forward and downward I lurched , dropping the saw onto my upper thigh.

There was no pain at first, and I thought I'd simply scratched myself. But when I looked more closely into the wound, I saw the dull gleam of my femur. Yet I was blessed that time too: the only female member of our party happened to be a nurse. While the men started tearing off their sleeves to stop the blood—there still wasn't much—she calmly instructed them to cut a pair of saplings for a makeshift splint: "We can't let that leg flex," she warned.

Later, after I'd taken a hundred stitches and even more staples, the surgeon told me something to make me shiver: "If you had bent your leg, the whole quadricep would have rolled up like a window shade, and you'd never walk right again."

I remember the two skinny lengths of maple propped in the corner as he spoke.

I make a lousy invalid, and I spent a grumpy three weeks after the event, unable to hike and hunt. But after that fairly short spell I grew sound as a dollar again.

In late summer of 2002, I had a siege of what my local G.P., a woman I like and admire greatly, noting the severe and increasing pains in all my joints, diagnosed as post-viral arthropathy, a condition often encountered by distance athletes. They might get some virus, usually a common cold, and sometimes one so mild they don't even notice it, and subsequently, this inflammatory process sets in. Now I had been rowing my shell and paddling my kayak in a sort of geezer mania in the preceding months, as much as fifteen miles a day on the gorgeous lakes near our Maine camp, so her sense of things seemed apt.

Two well regarded rheumatologists, one at Dartmouth and one at Brigham and Women's in Boston, suspected rheumatoid arthritis, but Melanie insisted my ailment would pass in due course. She monitored my dose of Prednisone, which I needed merely to get out of a chair, gradually diminishing it until the following June—at which point I went back to business as usual, none the worse for the experience.

During that stretch, I kept sermonizing myself: If you get out of this one, remember to be grateful for your good health. I also made a vow, more effective than the first, to sympathize with those who had no bodily soundness of their own, especially those who endured chronic pain.

Last summer, the only person to beat me in a long-distance, flat-water kayak race was a fellow less than half my age. I left all the others, each younger too, well in my wake. I suspect I owe such physical good fortune to my mother, who, despite her lifelong problems with alcohol, remained one of the toughest people I have ever known, a lady who celebrated her 74th birthday by trying out hang-gliding. She made it to 81, but Lord knows how long she'd have lasted without her mammoth daily doses of bourbon.

So yes, I have been blessed in my health, to the extent that I rarely think about it, let alone express gratitude to whatever power has guaranteed it. Such blitheness would have been unthinkable, however, from about my seventeenth year, when I left for college, through my late thirties. In that stretch, hypochondriac panic attacks would suddenly come upon me, without warning. I imagined cancer, heart failure (the more after my dad died at 56 from a coronary), inchoate blindness, liver disease, what have you? I sometimes had to cancel classes, simply because I was so frighteningly distracted by the imaginary ailment of the day.

Consultation with medical professionals didn't seem to help much. In college, doctors at the health service could barely conceal their contempt for this rather strapping late teenager who took up so much of their time. The mental health folks didn't do me a lot better: I did get anti-depressive medications, which mellowed me—until another panic attack came on. The one valuable thing that remains from my many hours in shrinks' offices were the words that one of them spoke: "I think you are afraid you won't measure up, and so you're looking for a chance to take a flop."

That makes perfect sense to me now; it didn't then, so it didn't help.

I have no real interest in psychology here, lacking both the training and the inclination. But, to say it tersely, I guess my worries over failure had something to do with the same mother.

It was, in a word, hard—no impossible—to measure up to her expectations, but I am long since over resentment about this, and many other things connected with the poor woman. I know that she was besieged by the terrible disease of addiction. And truth is, whether or not such a *Reader's Digest* evaluation of my youthful hypochondria holds water, my panic episodes faded, then vanished entirely, once I did begin to stack up some small accomplishments.

I worried myself to distraction back in a time when my health was a simple given; now that I'm of an age where health concerns will inevitably factor into my life, I worry not at all. I am rarely ill, and when I am, it's usually due to some 24-hour bug, which my body beats down in short order. But deep inside, of course, the urge to "take a flop" must endure, as I imagine it does for most. When I'm indulging in such a respite, when my excellent wife is seeing to my needs and, inert, I contemplate the lovely woods outside the bedroom window, I feel a strange but vaguely familiar serenity.

At such moments, there may come a memory, which has iconic value in my mental makeup—a sort of Ur-flop recollection, if you will. I'm about five and, as usual, have climbed into bed with my parents before they have gotten up. In time, also as usual, my father goes downstairs to make coffee. He will soon bring it back upstairs for my mother, who lolls beside me in her red velvet bed jacket. These are the sweetest recollections of her that I retain from our vexed relationship. I love the feel of that garment, and the odor of her hair, rank with sleep but sweet nonetheless.

Dad does reappear, with the dull metal perk pot and two cups on a tray. He apparently doesn't know that Colonel, his iron-blue hunting cocker, has followed him up and now stands at his knee, between him and bed. He can't see the dog for the tray in his hands. In an instant, he trips, and the steaming coffee spills onto my right arm.

I scream my lungs out, and my father is the very image of fuddled concern until Mom herself screams: "Call Tom!"

Dad dashes to the hall table and shakily dials a number taped up near the phone.

My pain seems to abate rather quickly. I lie with my back to a propped pillow and stare out the window. It has snowed heavily overnight: there's a small drift on the sill, and on the limbs of the window oak, through which the flakes softly tumble, mesmerizing, soporific.

Dad stands by another window, and after a spell, he says, "He's here." This was a long, long time before the SUV fad, so it must have taken some skill and experience—as I couldn't have recognized then—for the family doctor to drive his olive drab Chevy down the long hill from his home office to our house.

I've always felt affection for Dr. Tom, as I call him. It feels instinctive, as if he were a benign member of the family. The kindness of his face is genuine; I somehow know that for sure. He is tall and lank, with mere wisps of hair on top of his head. He is dressed, as ever, in a rumpled suit and the same rep tie, blue and red, the colors, I now realize, of his med school alma mater, the University of Pennsylvania. If I touch him anywhere, I believe, he will feel as soft as his own touch on my forehead or on my ear as he checks it for infection.

My parents have wrapped my arm in a wet towel. When the doctor removes it, on seeing the long blister, I tell Dr. Tom, "It looks like bubble gum." The sheet kind, I mean, Topps, with the baseball cards, not the tough squares of Fleer's Double Bubble or Bazooka (the latter of whose cartoon strips, featuring the laconic, turtle-necked Bazooka Joe, I prefer). Dad, obviously relieved by the doctor's presence and calm, laughs with him at the remark.

It's strange that I don't remember my mother during all of this. She must surely have been on hand, but that house call scene—in which the physician applies some gooey salve and wraps the wounded arm in gauze and tape—remains a very masculine one in mind, though the men are gentle.

"I'll come back after office hours to check him again," says Dr. Tom.

He adds that my father must call if such and such a development (I remember no details) ensues. But nothing untoward does ensue. Truth is, the middle hours of the day remain a blank in my recall.

Either the snow persists all day, or it has started again by the time the good doctor reappears. At all events, I can see flakes fluttering down past the yard light when he sits and unwraps the dressing, pronounces things well and good, and walks over to sit in one of two handsome Morris chairs.

My father has momentarily left the room, and when he returns, he bears the same tray. This time, though, it shows a bottle of whatever that brown stuff is my parents drink, two sturdy, short glasses, an ashtray and a pack of cigarettes.

For poets, there may be some dim surmise of a former paradise, an Elysium, a golden age, what have you? It plays at the verges of our consciousness, I think, even if we are, like me, realist authors, for lack of a preciser term.

Just so, the hypnotic snowfall, the comfort of Dad and Mom's bed, from which I haven't stirred since the morning accident, and the lazy drift of smoke above the two men: all these combine with the quiet conversation those old male friends are sharing to take me to the edge of sleep, and perhaps over that edge. Maybe in fact a good deal of that tableau may linger from dream.

No matter. Until my dying day, which if I dropped just now would be fourteen years later than that of my father, whose fatal heart attack caused a rift in my heart that has never really healed—until that last day, in mind I'll refer to the scene in my parents' bedroom as the archetypal example of peace, comfort and protection.

Who wouldn't willingly take a flop there?

RE: ILLNESS

Fleda—Staying Home from School

I LOVED BEING "SICK." If my body couldn't work up the germs, my mind could. Through grade school, all the way through high school, I was deft at turning a slightly scratchy throat into a wicked possible strep condition that would keep me home from school. To cinch the matter, I would vigorously rub the thermometer, or hold it under warm water at the bathroom sink when no one was looking, I don't know if my mother bought any of this, or if she was just too harried and/or depressed to fight me on it.

The half-year my aunt Cleone and her three wildly healthy boys lived with us in Columbia, I would be sick and my Aunt Cleone would position herself at my bedroom door, frowning. "Fleda, are you really sick enough to stay home?" she'd ask. She was onto me, which almost spoiled my day, but not quite.

Our house, in truth, was a house of illness. My brother was severely mentally retarded and had grand mal seizures so awful that each one would take your breath away. There was a heap of bottles, all full of potent drugs, on the kitchen counter, along with an apothecary's mortar and pestle to grind up the ones too difficult for him to swallow. My mother had severe arthritis—no wonder. My father had only allergies, but he was able to make a great deal out of lying on his back on the bed with his head over the side, dripping Neo-Synephrine into a stuffed-up nose. Don't get me wrong—we were also very physical. My mother loved to walk, arthritis or no. She could move really fast, her scarf tied under her chin like a

Russian peasant; my father rode his bike several miles to school when almost no one did such a thing; my sister and I rode bikes, swam, played rudimentary tennis, and walked. But it appears to me now that the one way I could be assured that my parents' attention would be directed at me was to be sick.

And also, I was shy —I guess you could call it that. In any case, I found being at home, being taken care of, very comforting. My mother would have liked to be a nurse and seemed to enjoy having me home, bringing me poached egg on toast, straightening my covers, finding the paper-doll pages in McCall's magazine for me, bringing me scissors and Scotch tape. The kid in Robert Louis Stevenson's "The Land of Counterpane" was me:

> When I was sick and lay a-bed,
> I had two pillows at my head,
> And all my toys beside me lay,
> To keep me happy all the day.

In fact, I remember lying there reading *A Child's Garden of Verses*. They were too young for me, but I loved them anyway. School was always pressure—get the math problems right, do well on the test, and carefully manage to fit into certain groups of friends. I think I was a bit afraid of people. Being alone felt safer, easier. There was often yelling and crying at home, that's true, but in the mornings when my father was at school, teaching, and my mother was putting around, taking care of Mark and washing clothes, the house was quiet, peaceful—her little radio in the kitchen tuned to the Arthur Godfrey show or whatever followed that.

One of the most reliable views out our front "picture" window was the Collier's Drug Store car pulling up to bring a delivery—a prescription or two plus anything else my mother could think of. She didn't drive and the delivery people were a major source of contact with the outside world. Years before that in Akron, Ohio, when I got measles, the doctor himself came to the house. Actually, in Arkansas that sometimes happened, too. Dr. Patrick didn't routinely do that by then—this would have been the late 1950s—but on occasion he would. He'd say he would stop by on his way home. I had mono when I was 15. I'm sure he came to the house more than once during my month-long isolation. The arrival of the doctor at our house was a solemn and dignified occasion, requiring the changing of bedcovers to prepare, the general straightening of things. He was the priest of the body. His deliberations, his manipulation of drugs, kept my brother's seizures under partial control. He held the keys. Besides, we were an isolated family, isolated in our relationships with the outside world, and he was one important link, maybe the most important.

I was a war baby, born just as manufactured drugs came into wide use. When I was very young, there were no antihistamines. I was taken to the doctor who put me on a table and used a bulb syringe to clear out my sinuses. "Say 'quack, quack, quack,'" he'd say as he sucked out what he could. Of course by the next day, I was right back in the same condition, unable to breathe. I had horrible earaches, with nothing to do for them but heating pads and soothing drops. Penicillin wasn't yet used often. I mostly suffered until my own body figured out how do deal with its invaders.

Compared to what was available in the 1950s, there are now drugs that work marvelously, efficiently, quickly. As the drug companies have turned out a wider variety of pills, and as the medical profession has available much more sophisticated tools—lasers, MRIs, CT scans, etc.—the role of the doctor, many have noted and lamented, has shifted from that of shaman to that of general contractor. The best of today's doctors—my present one included—work against this image, caring as much as they can, but most are hurried, worried about paying their own insurance bills, and overwhelmed with patients and paperwork. The doctor who stood at our bedside pronouncing the weighty words, "You'll be up and around in a week," has faded into Norman Rockwell paintings.

Being sick, for me, was a luxury. My daughter missed almost no school during her entire twelve years. Her delight and sustenance were her school friends. My son was a bit like me, but it wasn't as much fun to be home—home was often a tense and harried place to be. He did like to burrow under the covers with a book or a comic book, and sometimes had to be persuaded that he wasn't as sick as all that.

I will tell about my month at home with mono when I was in the tenth grade, because it will give you some idea of the pleasure of being sick. The shades were to be drawn. I was not to have sunlight. I was to stay in bed. My temperature was to be taken regularly. I was to have plenty of fluids. I was absolved from the world, essentially, at a time when the world was becoming a huge complication for me. Toward the end, friends were allowed to visit, but I was to stay quiet when they came. Two friends delivered my homework assignments to me, and of course I had all my school books at home. I would work for a while, propped up in bed, before I got sleepy and put it all aside. This was the great pleasure, putting things aside. Certainly, the drumbeat of responsibility sounded quietly from the bookcase where my assignment sheets lay. But I could ask for orange juice and it would arrive. I would take a bath and when I returned to bed, my mother would have put on nice, clean sheets.

As the month wore on, the drumbeat got louder and my restlessness got more pronounced. I began to fear returning to school. It was a scary day when I actually did walk to the bus stop and stand in the cold with my friends. And each classroom was, for me that day, an exercise in terror—how would I catch up with what could not be extracted from written lessons? How would I fit back in when the waters appeared to have closed around my absence?

In a family where illness rules, where it's always present, there is a sense of stagnation, of a holding pattern. My brother would never grow up and would never be well. How could the body be counted on to behave as it should, when in this glaring case, it didn't and wouldn't? There was a fascination in my family with how the body was behaving on any particular day. We were not exactly a family of hypochondriacs—we loved the outdoors and being active too much for that—but we were certainly interested in the mechanics of the body.

I think this was particularly true because my father—as I diagnose him after all those years of not having a clue—was on the milder end of autistic. His emotional responses were elicited only by the concrete. If we wanted his attention, wanted him to focus on something having to do with ourselves, all we had to do was claim to be sick and/or in pain. The tangible world, he understood. When I was eleven, I was sewing doll clothes on the floor with my sister. I stuck the needle in the rug for a minute, and then forgot about it and crawled across the rug after a scrap of material. The needle went deep into my knee, broke off in the bone. If I moved my knee even a millimeter, I screamed with pain. In the doctor's office, my father stood over me as the doctor probed and dug around to get the needle out. My father had to leave the room to keep from throwing up, he said later. THIS was real attention. He was in sympathy with me. I was actually proud of pain that would elicit this from him.

Fortunately, blessedly, except for my aging knees and back, nothing much hurts me these days. I am rarely sick. On those few occasions when I feel bad enough to flop myself into bed and pull up the covers, for a brief time I am back there: warm, taken care of, the center of attention, and cut loose from the heavy world. Briefly. No one would wish for it to be longer than that.

Postscript: I read this last paragraph with sadness and a sense of irony. Not long after I wrote those words, I was diagnosed with cancer that had metastasized. I've had the full run of chemo and radiation. If I follow the lines of this essay, would I have to say that I brought this on? Not on your life. I have a good life, and work that I'm eager to continue. I'm happy. I don't want to stay home from school any more. Ted Kooser, our former poet U. S. poet laureate who's been through this himself, told me, "You will be more in love with your life than ever when this is all over."

I don't know how I could be more in love with it, I wrote back.

WILD ANIMALS

Fleda—Mildred

HOW DID WE CHOOSE "'WILD Animals"? Wildness as what's disappearing? Wildness as the uncontrollable stream that runs through a poem, something like the musk of felt life? We glorify the primal hypothalamus, the direct shot of adrenaline, as if it's more "true" than our contemplative cerebral cortex. This is understandable; we miss our animals as more and more become extinct. We miss our material world as it seems to move farther from our fingers. We miss ourselves as we live more and more in our thoughts instead of our bodies. I miss Mildred. I haven't seen her in a long while. This is her story.

When she comes to the water, we don't see her. We don't see her when she goes. We hear the splashing, we see the paw-prints, the five long claws. She lives under the cottage. We see where she enters. With our allusive and complicated brains, we decide to make her stand for what was there before we were. She is probably not the same raccoon. They live only one to three years. We give her an imagined continuity. We name her Mildred after Mildred Osborne, the now-deceased next door neighbor, for no reason other than to keep the Osbornes around a while longer, although the new people, new for the last ten years, are better neighbors, that is, they take the kids out on their jet skis and fast boat, which we refuse to own, ourselves.

Mildred has babies in our cottage crawl space. John, the carpenter remodeling our kitchen, says he hears scuttling and scuffling above his head. Our other neighbor, Lou, says we should set a trap to catch "Mildred" and drown her. There are too many "Mildreds" getting into trash buckets, he says. John says we should get poison or something. Or shoot her. I think maybe my sensitivity is too precious for their older world. I think of my father and his brother, out with their shotguns killing crows, squirrels, anything that came along, as if the world would last forever. I remember his tilting the leftover paint thinner toward the water, pausing as I yelled, "No! Not in the water!" and his reply, "Oh for Pete's sake, it's only a little!" The signals sent out by the struggling world had not yet reached him. Or he wasn't listening. When he was young, what was a little kerosene in the water? Who wouldn't clean paint brushes there? He was only one generation removed from the clear-cutting of the northern forests for timber. When his parents bought the cottage, there were only a few young trees starting back around the lake—the old ones had been felled and floated to the sawmill.

Maybe it's not fair of me about the shotgun. We kill animals in much worse ways now. We cage them and murder them by machine. We eat them without having any sense of the reality of the living, breathing presence of the animal we're eating. There's no fairness, no contest of gun and human wit against animal stealth and sharp senses.

I call the SPCA. The young woman tells me they can't come get a raccoon. She tells me to soak a rag in ammonia and to play loud music near the crawl space to drive her out.

I forgot to say Mildred got into the cottage by crawling down the chimney. And then up the stairs. I think I will drive her out, then crawl in and get her babies, put them in a box, and take them to a place where she can move them elsewhere. I soak the rag and set it just inside the crawl space. I can see nothing in there, in the dark. I get my little red radio and tune in the loudest music, which turns out to be Christian rock. All night in my sleep or semi-sleep, the Christians are letting me know they are here, and up to date.

The morning mist is rising and there is Mildred pacing the roof of the cottage. She sees me. I imagine she sees me although raccoons have very poor distance vision. Maybe she senses me. We look in each other's direction for a long minute, two mothers who have responsibilities that wrack our bodies, that hold us to our bodies, to all of our bodies, to the body of the world, no matter what. We know each other. We know nothing of each other. I continue with my plan. I block the opening to the fireplace. I get a cardboard box. I go upstairs and open the crawl space. It is very dark in there. There is loud scuffling and hissing and miniature growling beyond the range of my flashlight. I don't know how old the babies are. They may be almost ready to leave the nest. They may have grown very sharp claws and teeth. I back out of the crawlspace. I take the ammonia-soaked rag with me. I have already turned off the music, which was still blasting in Jesus' name.

I go downstairs and remove the piece of steel that we use to close up the fireplace in winter. I set aside the bucket I used to hold it tight against the fireplace opening. I go back out in the woods and watch the roof, where Mildred is still pacing. I tell her without speaking that she can go back in. I tell her I give up. She lumbers to the chimney and slowly lowers herself. I don't know how she knows except maybe the draft of air rising now. I am anthropomorphizing to claim she understands me. We are mortal enemies who read the signals, each of us, to save our skin. When she is all the way in the chimney, she stops and looks at me again before she lowers herself out of sight.

I'm trembling with the suddenness of the transition, with my sudden change of heart. I call it that, imagining that Mildred sees it as that, as my magnanimity, but is really only fear, which is certainly the other side of desire. Desire is reaching toward as well as trying to avoid. Pulling toward or away. I understand that these are the twin engines that try to keep us going forever. It does not matter that I understand this. Mildred is gone the next day, and has taken her babies with her.

I tried to write a poem about her, about that time. I'd say it was a failure. Often the most dramatic moments, the ones loaded with narrative and image and intensity, the ones that people say, "You should write a poem about this!" don't work out for me. I've written many narrative poems that seem pretty successful, but I think it's that they snuck up on the narrative. It's the head-on effort that defeats the poem. Maybe it's the idea of "poem" taking precedence over the moment itself, that freezes the moment so it can't open to the unknown. Maybe the telling gets to sounding like a braggart in a bar. Not enough reverence for the actual and true.

Someday I may find that I've approached Mildred from an angle where she can't see me and maybe I can't see her. There will be a furry shadow that goes somewhere I wouldn't have thought. That will be the poem. That will be the real Mildred.

RE: WILD ANIMALS

Syd—Unskunked

I LOATHE AND, LARGELY ON BEHALF of the animals, have always campaigned against the Disneyfied anthropomorphization of wildlife, though of course I am scarcely immune from such silliness myself. Closer to immune, perhaps, than most, but still susceptible. On which more as I go along, but first I turn to skunks.

Many, many years ago I wrote a poem called "The Feud." It got a little acclaim, several commentators applauding my re-importation of elements that poetry had for some while largely ceded to fiction: character, plot, setting, dialogue—values of that sort.

In fact I hadn't set out with any agenda in mind. I'd come to poetry late in life by most people's standards, having been a conventional academic into my mid-thirties, and I didn't know much about contemporary poetry. (I'm not yet sure I do.) So I wasn't looking to be idiosyncratic or aesthetically inventive. I merely wanted to tell a tale, and when I did it presented itself in blank verse for some reason.

"The Feud" is a long poem, some seventeen typescript pages, so it may appear surprising that it came to me entire in less than an hour. I never stopped my fingers on the keyboard, wrote as if possessed. Thereafter, I did revise the poem some, but very minimally: I remember excising one stanza of the many, for example, and changing a handful of words here and there. But that was more or less it.

I now think "The Feud's" sudden arrival had something to do with its being the first thing I wrote in the half-year following the shocking death by aneurysm of my younger brother. That event, of course, made me wonder among other things why in the world one would bother with mere poetry. I'm now persuaded that the whole story of "The Feud" is allegorical of my relationship with the man who'd died so tragically young, which was at once an intimate and a heatedly adversarial relationship, one on which I had of course been meditating for those six months, even when I didn't know it. In short, I had been doing so much emotional research that when I began composition, the material was right at my fingertips.

My narrative involved a speaker and his hostile dealings with a local have-not family named Walker. That speaker is proud unto vain, and is especially given to righteousness: throughout the tale, he contrasts himself with his sad, impoverished counterparts, seeing respectable ideals in himself, and in them none whatsoever.

I didn't like my protagonist much, I still don't, but it took me more than a year after the poem's completion to recognize why: his self-absorption and quickness to judge were a lot like my own, particularly with respect to my late brother. I considered my roles as scholar and athlete to be exemplary; he thought they were useless charades. And despite certain of my shortcomings in her eyes, to my mother too I was white sheep, he black.

I look back on that sad period and I understand why I might have had a negative opinion of myself in those days. It wasn't only my scores of petty feuds with the younger brother, which seemed so ridiculously petty in the wake of his passing. I can't list, either, all the times I fabricated occasions to look down on colleagues, neighbors, dear friends and even family.

Let me try to make sense of this somewhat diffuse preamble. Its musings arise from the fact that, having read of Fleda's adventures with an invasive raccoon, when I thought about my own confrontations with wild animals (and as an inveterate and devoted hunter I have of course had countless ones), I somehow thought of a passage from "The Feud," and I recalled, scarcely for the first time, the circumstances that engendered that passage.

"The Feud's" speaker at one point refers to a time when a skunk, reacting to a rush from his house cat, sprayed copiously in a shed under his bedroom: "The smell was worse than death," he asserts,

> And till the dawn arrived, for hours I felt
> the stink was like a judgment: every sin
> from when I was a child till then flew back
> and played itself again before my eyes.

Now the closest encounter I've ever had with skunks goes back to when I was more or less a child. Fourteen years old, I was mowing a patch of meadow at my great uncle's farm. Suddenly the tractor's sickle bar decapitated a mother skunk, though it was set high enough to pass over the heads of her three small kits.

I don't know where on earth I could have gotten the notion, but I somehow believed—given their tininess—the baby skunks were too young to spray. I left them tumbling between windrows and ran to the barn for a burlap sack. I'd heard that skunks made good pets, and my animal-loving mother, I figured, would surely pay to have their musk sacs removed before their defensive mechanisms became, as it were, operational. I hustled back, holding the bag open and reaching for the first kit.

In that instant, all three small skunks fell quickly into formation and blasted me from less than two feet away.

I won't speak for others, but I find the distant smell of skunk almost pleasant, wild and woodsy as it is, redolent, particularly, of spring. To be literally soaked in skunk musk is another matter entirely. Child of the 60s, I know what tear gas is like, but give me a choice between the gas and what I experienced on that morning over fifty years ago, and I'll opt for the cops and canisters.

Choking, blinded, I bumbled to the pond and threw myself in—which of course did no good at all. I have since learned that women's douching solution is a fine antidote for skunk, and we now keep a lot of it on hand for dog-vs.-skunk emergencies. But I didn't know this unlikely remedy then. I submitted to a more traditional one: my bachelor great uncle's wise and wonderful Irish housekeeper (God bless dear Mary Griffin) doused me with tomato juice, tomato paste, even ketchup, which made things not perfect but a lot better. I soaked in a bubbly bathtub through the afternoon, then took shower after shower, slathered myself with my great uncle's cologne, and by evening, I'd become bearable to Mary—and to myself.

For weeks after, however, when the weather turned very humid or rainy, the odor of skunk came nauseatingly back, and I recall that for whatever reason, yes, "the stink was like a judgment."

Now let me leap ahead some twenty years, to the time when I lived in that drafty yellow farmhouse with my first wife. One August, two or three times a week a certain skunk kept waddling into the shed below our bedroom, even after I moved our rubbish can down-cellar. Having struck pay dirt once, it seemed, the beast imagined that with persistence he'd get lucky again.

We had a cat named Wendy, good in the house but in many ways half feral. We left her outdoors at night all year round, and in summer would simply let her fend for herself back home after we went to our Maine camp for almost a month. She was always sleek and fat when we returned, having subsisted on the plentiful voles and red squirrels of the remote neighborhood. Wendy charged that skunk each time it came calling, but somehow managed never to get sprayed herself. The stench would rise up, though, and would indeed awaken us.

One night, an unusually hot and steamy one for upper New England, I lay sleeping in the buff on top of the bedclothes. When the smell came on, I swore I'd had enough. Rushing down to my hunting room, I fetched my double-barreled 12-gauge Winchester, a handful of shells and a flashlight. Then I ran to the kitchen door that opened into the shed.

The animal must somehow have sensed danger, because, under a hazy full moon, I saw it bobbing as fast as it knew how down the dirt road, about to reach the deep woods west of the house. I knew I'd never catch the skunk on foot. Of course, a skunk is not speedy, but he had a hundred yards on me already. So I leapt into my old Chevy pickup and roared after it, leaning out the window, shotgun in my left hand, ready to lean out and blow the creature to kingdom come, like one of my childhood cowboy heroes shooting from horseback.

Just as I came within range, ready to hit the brakes and fire, I lost control of the truck and fishtailed into the woods myself. I miraculously avoided every tree, but, four-wheel drive be damned, I found myself hopelessly stuck in a wetland pothole.

So there was I, buck naked, toting a shotgun, that full hundred yards and more from my house. Thank God, I thought, we live in the middle of nowhere and it's three in the morning. I started walking homeward.

And then I heard the engine. Unbelievably, on looking back I saw headlights pointing upward; whoever it may have been was climbing the hill a quarter mile west of me, headed my way. By now I was out in the meadowland, so I couldn't just dash back into the forest for cover. Instead, I stumbled up into a field and lay my naked body on the stubble of lately cut hay, mosquitoes strafing me, astonished, or so I fancied, by their good fortune.

To make matters worse, the driver of the car—whose identity I'll never know—had noticed my truck in the woods and, no doubt with the best of intentions, gotten out to inspect the scene of the accident. I heard male voices, though not at such a distance what they were saying.

Jesus, can't they see there's no one there? I inwardly screamed. The would-be Samaritan seemed to be lingering a long, long time, and

I was in plain misery there on my painful bed, easy prey for the vicious insects.

In due course, the vehicle passed, I picked myself up, returned to the house, showered, went back to bed. But I never slept again through those long, early morning hours. Again, "the stink was like a judgment." I lay there in a stew, wondering how in hell I had turned out to be such an unadmirable man. My every peccadillo seemed monstrous. Insomnia can have that effect under the best of conditions.

Even now I wonder why, after those three skunk kits let me have it at fourteen, I'd felt so unlikable too.

In the psycho-babble parlance of our time, I do have a tendency—as my wife often reminds me—to low self-esteem, and although I don't want to engage in psycho-babble myself, I suspect that this self-laceration goes back to my twisty relationship with that same animal-loving mother.

I was a good student back in the field-mowing days, and better later along, but I never proved good enough for mom. An example: our school still used a numbered grading system, and I recall getting a 96 on my English final in tenth grade. I also vividly recall her asking me what had happened to the other four points. For all I know, she was joking—but I'm guessing not.

It was late in her quite productive but highly troubled life that she told me something about her own school days, something I believe to be crucial, determinative. She was her class valedictorian, and had just been accepted to Radcliffe, about the toniest women's college going at the time. When she ran with the news to her uncle, the same one whose field I mowed and who was my mother's virtual father, her biological one having died in her fifth year—when she ran in, breathless, to share that report from Radcliffe, he looked her in the eye and said five terse words.

Women don't go to college.

I am sure the man carried his bag of rocks too. My siblings and I have wondered since if he remained unmarried because he was gay, closeted as the times demanded, but there is no way to prove that either way. He could be gracious and generous, and he could also be explosive. Most frightening, however, was when he turned steely.

Women don't go to college. On hearing that pronouncement, my mother must instantly have known there'd be no appeal.

And so, I believe, she expected me to be her academic surrogate. She may well have withheld approval of my scholastic achievements out of a belief that, though I'd been given the opportunity summarily denied to her, they amounted to relatively little. It seems never to have occurred to her that I was doing the best I could. Who knows? Maybe I wasn't. But that is a separate story.

After my mother's death, and after more a decade of resenting her memory, I wrote her a letter whose first half catalogued all my grievances, the second half cataloguing the things she'd passed on for which I felt grateful. I went to the columbarium where her remains lay, read the letter aloud, then struck a match to the paper, watching its ashes fall to the earth around her own. For whatever reason, the resentments vanished in the instant.

My feelings about myself have subsequently improved, at however gradual a rate.

Which, oddly, brings me to skunks yet again. I recall a beautiful forenoon in May, and my wonderful wife and I enjoying it in Montreal's botanical gardens. We had gone to that great city for a romantic weekend, and the blue sky, the brilliant sun, and the countless flowers in bud or bloom all felt perfectly in tune with that mission.

We were near the Japanese temple at the heart of the gardens when my wife noticed a rustling in some ground ivy.

"What do you suppose that is?" she asked.

We leaned over together as I parted the leaves. There stood the skunk, back to, tamping its front feet, its spray-hole distended almost to bursting. Needless to say, we bolted like hares.

As we walked back to the subway, we marveled at our good luck. Once sprayed, we'd never have been allowed on that Métro; we couldn't have hailed a cab; it was a full five-mile hike back to the hotel, and once we got there, we'd have been barred from entering too. What in the world might we have done?

Why that little creature didn't let us have it I will never know. But while my love and I wandered along, I gradually realized that I felt not a trace of the old self-loathing. Perhaps that equanimity came only from not being sprayed by that skunk. And yet there's still enough of the romantic poet in me to turn that fact around.

As I said at the start, I am profoundly hostile to the sentimental humanization of wild things, the imputing to beasts the sort of interpretative capacities that we men and women (think we) have. So I know full well how wrong the following notion is on a literal level. Metaphorically, however, it makes perfect sense to me that the skunk failed to spray simply because I'm a different man at seventy than I was at thirty or even fourteen—a man who, in his own eyes at least, has a lot less to feel guilty or inadequate about.

SPORTS

Fleda—Trapped by Rules

YOU WANT TO TALK ABOUT SPORTS? Oh dear, this is your
subject, I assure you, not mine! Neither of my parents cared
a whit for sports. Oh, my mother claimed to be interested in the
Missouri Tigers, as a nod to her beloved father, who had season
tickets for years. No one taught me to play any team sports. When
I was chosen for a baseball team in—what?—it must have been
second or third grade, I had no idea what to do. I tried to fake it,
but I didn't know how to hold a bat, or what base was what. After
that, I got a knot in my stomach when someone said, "Hey, let's play
baseball." I did learn basketball, of course, in gym class. I liked the
fast movement, the dip and dive, the aim and shoot. It was all pretty
much fun, as far as gym class went.

When I entered high school, I wanted more than anything to
be chosen to be a "Pepper." I cared nothing about football, but
everyone who was anyone was a Pepper. You got to wear a purple
pleated skirt and white sweater with a purple bulldog on it. You got
to walk onto the field in a line and sit all together in the bleachers,
raising your pompom and shaking it in sync with the others at first
downs and touchdowns. I had no clue what a first down was, but
I learned to yell at the right time, and I definitely liked shaking the
pompoms.

And then for a few years, I taught high school. Imagine me at
Springdale High School, on the court. We'd staged a teacher's

basketball game, the bleachers filled with our students. I had the ball. Crowd roars. I run the wrong direction.

A couple of years later, however, I sat in the bleachers quite happily with my then-husband, who was a part-time sports writer for the local newspaper. He told me what to watch for, and, willing for anything to be material, I wrote a poem called "Goat" about a pitcher who walks the batter.

I have sat quite happily since with my beloved husband of twenty-one years, staring mindlessly at a baseball game on TV, or trying to read while he watches and rubs my feet. I've eaten hot dogs and stared dreamily into space sitting beside him on the bleachers at Camden Yards or what used to be called Veterans Stadium in Philadelphia. To date, I've written two sports poems. Just to prove to you I can do it, here is the second one, written entirely, of course, with information fed to me by my husband. It's in my book, *Breathing In, Breathing Out,* from Anhinga Press, 2001.

Cosmic Pitching

Fidrych would lift his wild golden curls
and talk to the sky. Hrabosky the same,
and he'd talk to the ball, circling
the mound, face twitching. And then he would
face the centerfield fence, whirl back
around, go into his stretch, and
pitch.
       It's best not to take chances. You
get your mind stalking and empty.
You slap your glove on your thigh, pace
your pattern. You make a ring of not-caring
around the thing. Too much pressure on one
point and the energy's down a black hole.
Carlton, on the watch for UFOs, what he might
have been doing is picking up an
archipelago as it moved through its
calculations. His mind was just breathing
in and out.
       So much that's far-fetched
lodges between the in and the out.

Did I mention Luis Tiant, flinging his
head to the sky as his arm came down?
Proof that the center of the world is in
the body, not the sight. You get these actions
together that don't care about each other.
They don't stand for anything.
                    Listen, ball.
Bless you, ball. You and I, ball.
You get into a rhythm. Inside the rhythm
is a pitch. You keep your mind on the
rhythm, waiting to feel the pitch coming on.
You don't know how to speak directly to
the thing you want more than anything.

I sound as if I know something, don't I? Well, okay, it's not so much
about the game as about writing, and about all things we have to
approach from an oblique angle, to know at all.

Board games. I'm not fond of them, either. Too bad, since games
are a great way to keep an activity going and make conversation
easier with grandchildren, for example. I learned to play bridge
once, and poker, with my first husband. When we were students, we
had some good enough evenings with friends over a bridge game,
with pizza from a box mix and a jug of Gallo wine. But I would've
given anything if someone had said, "Let's skip the game and just
sit and talk." Games make me feel the way piano lessons did, fenced
in, trapped by rules. Too bad, because if I hadn't had such a need
to escape rules, I might have developed discipline a lot earlier. It
took serious academic pressure—the Ph.D. program—to get me to
buckle down and stay with the rules of the game until I finished.
Not accidentally, no doubt, my poems improved a great deal during
that time.

Wouldn't it be nice if free verse were really, as Frost said, like playing
tennis without a net? Every move we make on paper brings along
with it a set of rules for what's next. Tradition or not, regular form
or not, there is always the needs of one word, of one line, to answer
to. Nothing's free.

But I can pretend. I'm good at pretending there are no rules. Here is a list of my pretendings:

(1) My stand-up paddleboard. I tie a big scarf around my waist and I'm Cleopatra, poling down the Nile. I'm pretty sure she didn't do that, but if she had, it would've been like this. I love the solitary swish of water. I like to go out in early morning or late evening, when the lake is still and the water's a mirror barely dividing me from the other world.

(2) Swimming. My parents loved swimming. And biking, and what we called walking, which has been professionalized into "hiking" these days. I was following along on their long walks when my legs were too short to keep up for long. My father pulled the little red wagon to give me a rest, or he sat me on his shoulders until I was ready to walk again. There was no such thing as a "destination." The idea was exploration and the sheer joy of movement. I spent my childhood roaming creek beds as far as I was allowed to go, climbing over rocks, digging for beetles, sticking sticks in anthills, and climbing trees along the way. I have been in love with motion of my own choosing, at my own pace and time.

It seems necessary now to have special clothes, special equipment, for what used to seem normal activities, what you did to have fun. You did not have hiking boots. You did not have a pedometer. You did not keep track. You just had a good time.

(3) My bike. I could not wait to have my own bike. I didn't get to have one my size. My father bought a used one way too big for me and put blocks on the pedals. I had no helmet, no gears, no odometer. All my young years, the bike invisibly clocked invisible time, invisible distance. It was repainted deep blue, banged up a bit on the fenders. Its only accessory was a big basket on the handlebars for books and such. I would ride until it was too dark to see where I was going. I would ride in the mist of early summer mornings before it got hot. I would push my legs as hard as they would go up the long, steep Garland Avenue to my friend Donna's house. I did not measure myself by an instrument, but by my father, who could

make it up the hill without getting off and walking the bike. I was thirteen. I made it.

(4) A rowboat. Not just any rowboat. The flat bottom kind is no good for anything. You need to have a slight keel to keep from wasting your stroke with sideways slippage. We had a flat bottom one, which was relegated to whichever kids reached the boats last. Or the youngest, hence without power. We had a glorious double-oared rowboat (a Whitehall, I find out later), that my cousin Alan and I would row the mile to town so fast we made a wake. Then we would hang along the shore, watching for turtles. Alan was bigger and stronger, although we were the same age. I measured myself by how perfectly I could keep up with his strokes. We were a big green dragonfly, skimming the water for the pure pleasure of it, of using our muscles, of seeing how far and fast we could go on our own energy without stopping for rest.

(5) Canoes. The way they slip through the water without letting you know it. I love the way you're sitting straight-backed, tilting your paddle down with a J-stroke, correcting yourself with each stroke. I love their silence most of all, as if they are only a breath on the water. Like my paddleboard, I love them on the margins of the day, when the big boats tire of roaring aimlessly up and down and go home to recoup.

(6) Kayaks. There are two little ones, yellow and green. I take the green one when I want to be invisible. I take the yellow one when I want to be sure the big boats see me. I like to paddle down to the lily pads, where the turtles are, and where a heron lives. If I slide along quietly enough, the turtles will stay on their logs. I have followed the heron as she walked down the shoreline simultaneously alert and easy, as if she didn't have a care in the world.

(7) Sailboats. Well, I kind of love sailboats. I can tolerate a sailboat, I should say. I prefer not to be at the mercy of wind, stalled in the middle of the lake in beating sun, but there's always the sloop-slurp of waves on the side of the boat, the thrill of the gust that suddenly drives us forward, the taut sail, the outward lean to balance.

In general, you could say I'm a failure at all games. I am willing to play Scrabble or Monopoly with grandchildren on a rainy day at the cottage, if every other possibility is exhausted. I choose my shiny metal car and collect my money. I start out with as much attention as I can manage, cheering for myself when I get out of jail, when I'm able to buy a house on Boardwalk. But the thrill of acquisition palls, the tedium of circling the board overtakes me. I realize this game is going to last into the next generation, at least till the end of the summer. I start thinking of things I urgently need to do: the roast in the oven, the clothes out of the dryer. I call for as many breaks as I can get away with. Every person who walks by, I generously offer my place at the table. I am seldom taken up on my offer. I almost always lose the game. I try to pay attention, I really do. I try to want to win. I do not want to win. I want to break through underbrush, climb, float, paddle, swim. By myself or not. I like people, I really do. I like them best one by one. It is the space around us I love, holding us loosely, no lines, no goalposts, no ball.

RE: SPORTS

Syd: Suicidal Beauty

MY CASE, AS YOU KNOW, is far different from yours, Fleda, and no matter the slight self-contempt such a feeling engenders, my love of sports abides—if love is the accurate word.

At my age, in most cases I am perforce a spectator, one soul among the millions of other fans out there; and yet to witness or even to think of athletic competition means for me the electrification of some deep and inscrutable nerve. One cause of this enduring spark must surely be a certain now-ancient headline. I'll never forget it:

LEA AND HARMAR STAR IN UPSET OF HOTCHKISS

The banner ran in the local newspaper after our ragtag club team beat the prep school with the longstanding hockey tradition. None of us had expected other than a humbling defeat. If I had to count up ten "peak" experiences in my life, at least my younger life, that game, and the way I played it, would make the list, whatever such a fact may imply about my character.

Over the years, to repeat an abiding motif, I have perhaps too often inclined to consider myself a merely okay sort of person, not just as athlete but also as scholar, father, husband, poet, what have you? In my school days, I was proficient with languages and with words in general; indeed, I was a high-end student in all the humanities; but as soon as someone introduced abstract scientific concepts or even plain numbers into the conversation, my game was over. Thus, while I always made my school's honor roll, I never quite reached high honors.

Now I am poet laureate of Vermont, which has been a great treat: I've roamed my little state, library to library, reading and discoursing, and inevitably met up with intriguing people.

A few months back, for instance, in a postage stamp town, a farmer walked over after my presentation and showed me a book: *Mountain Interval,* by Robert Frost. He asked if I knew it, and I truthfully said indeed I knew its poems well.

"How many of them can you say?" he asked.

I told him I could probably do two or three entire.

"I can do 'em all," he answered.

I quizzed him, not asking for recitations of famous entries like "The Road Not Taken" but ones like "Pea Brush" or "An Encounter."

He obviously had the entire volume by heart.

That sort of experience has made my honorific position a joy. And yet sometimes at night I hear a voice (is it my mother's or my own, or are those one and the same?): "Poet Laureate of Vermont? What about the U.S.?"

Meandering seems almost a hobby, and I have wandered from that hockey game, in which I played right defense, Billy Harmar left. I was a good player, maybe more than merely good; Billy, on the other hand, a genuine star, would go on to play professionally in the Eastern Hockey League before deciding to take his life in other directions. Who knows how far up he might have gone from there if he'd chosen? He was brilliant.

For that one night, however, I was brilliant too, and I felt it. I will always have that game to refer to, even if I've likely never again felt the rush of fulfillment to quite the same degree, at least certainly not on an athletic stage.

To be sure, I've known periods of writing that, whatever others may think about the results, have felt somewhat akin. In those spans, I have come as close to believing in inspiration as I ever will: my fingers move on the keyboard as though they were being guided by something outside myself; my "moves," to revert to sporting terms, appear to be given to me.

On the evening when Billy and I starred against that daunting team of visitors, everything I did also seemed determined by a power beyond me, and every move went right. I recall, for example, making a rush on goal from the blue line, then sweeping the puck behind me to Billy, who slapped a hard shot at the cage. In the same instant, I saw the Hotchkiss goalie in position to catch the puck, so I held my stick in its path and ticked it just enough to send it over his glove hand.

Billy had a stunningly fast shot. I'm persuaded I couldn't have replicated that deflection once in ten further tries.

But what I remember most is a certain face-off. I simply knew that the puck, exactly at the moment the ref dropped it, would fly my way belt-high. I held my gauntleted right hand, which I'd normally have kept on the stick, right at the proper level to snare that puck and in the same second drop it and pass it cross-ice to a teammate, who led a scoring charge up to the other goal.

Between periods, our own first-rate goalie, Tom Lewis—now an eminent scholar and my dear friend of more than sixty years, the two of us having gone to nursery school together—said, "It must have been premonition, the way you reached for that puck."

It was just that, but where the foreknowledge came from will forever be a mystery.

The next year I got admitted to Yale, where, I was assured, all the students would be geniuses, to which I can tersely respond by mentioning a name: George W. Bush. Be that as it may, there were some very bright young men on the New Haven campus. There were also some exceptionally good hockey players.

I knew I'd never be the best student in my class, any more than I'd be the best player on the hockey team. And so, utterly uncertain as to who the hell the real Lea was, I must have concluded that I'd be the best hard-drinking, partying, outrageous good student and good hockey player anyone knew.

I didn't know it at seventeen, but I was already on my way to a years-long, dazing battle with substance abuse, mostly alcohol. I saw no problem even when, in due course, the addictive demons taking over, my grades turned from highly respectable to B and lower. Eventually, it seems almost unnecessary to add, I quit the hockey squad.

I never, however, entirely quit my enthusiasm for sports. When I got to grad school, and soon enough started my college teaching career I turned myself into a fine handball player, though there remained people, like the greatly decent and greatly skilled Dartmouth intramural coach Will Volz, to whom I remained an agonizing touch inferior.

It was thus almost a relief when, in 1975, a torn meniscus—treatment for which was far dicier and debilitating than it is in our era of arthroscopic surgery—got in the way, and I had to quit that competition too.

From childhood, of course, I'd had other sporting instincts, ones of a different stripe. I loved to train and hunt behind bird dogs; I loved to fly fish; I loved hiking and canoeing. These have, in fact, remained lifelong passions, to which I have added kayaking, something, as I mentioned earlier, that I've occasionally practiced competitively in the last half decade. All these pursuits keep me in pretty fair shape, especially since I got into recovery from addiction some considerable time back. So far as team sports go, though, I am now not unlike many more sedentary friends: I don't watch TV news, sitcoms, or anything else. But I do watch sports.

Perhaps oddly, I do not follow the favorite sport of my youth: this may simply be any old fogey's rumination, but it doesn't seem to me that the teamwork, especially the passing, is what it was in the era of Maurice Richard, Jean Beliveau, Red Kelly and Doug Harvey. Modern players seem simply to dump the puck into the offensive zone and then go racing after it. And the glorification of fights—though I concede I had my share of them in my playing days—now strikes me as anything but glorious.

If I'm at home, however, rarely do I miss either a Celtics or Red Sox game, no matter I was anything but adept at either of those games. I spectate alone for the most part, and would be, in all candor, a tad embarrassed to have other grown men and women regard the passion of my rooting.

Yes, I am a gung-ho fan, even if I know how silly it is to heroize athletes of any stripe, let alone the pros, whose ranks include so many undesirables: narcissists at best, referring to themselves in the third person, others wife-beaters, felons, and cheats, imagining themselves immune from the societal and characterological strictures that the rest of us must accept. If there are heroic figures in sports—I think of Jackie Robinson, say, or Stan Musial or Bill Russell—I fear they are the exceptions.

Of course, it's not merely the athletes who so often disgrace themselves. As I write this, football's New Orleans Saints are under scrutiny for something called Bountygate, their former defensive coach having offered pay to players who injured other teams' stars. It revolts me to know that there are those who excuse this pig's incentives, as if the potential ruin of an opponent's career, or the permanent alteration of his health, were just—as they say—"a part of the game."

Football, I admit, is my least favorite of the major sports, and my attitude toward most football coaches I have observed ranges from contempt to mere neutrality. To me it is telling that the NFL's Super Bowl trophy is named for someone who famously claimed that "winning isn't the most important thing; it's the only thing." To some, these are words of an inspiring figure; to me they are those of a moral idiot. Wouldn't the world be well served by abandoning such primitive counsel?

And yet.

And yet here is a challenging poem by James Wright called "Autumn Begins in Martin's Ferry, Ohio":

> In the Shreve High football stadium,
> I think of Polacks nursing long beers in Tiltonsville,
> And gray faces of Negroes in the blast furnace at Benwood,
> And the ruptured night watchman of Wheeling Steel
> Dreaming of heroes.
>
> All the proud fathers are ashamed to go home.
> Their women cluck like starved pullets,
> Dying for love.
>
>
> Therefore,
> Their sons grow suicidally beautiful
> At the beginning of October,
> And gallop terribly against each other's bodies.

A quick and careless reading of that poem would go something like this: the world of Martin's Ferry is arid, oppressive, sexually deprived, and as a result—note that the word therefore is the only one with its own line—the community's blighted adults make heroes of their athletic male children, who, we know, will succeed them in their own ruined domain.

But where is the speaker of this poem, the poet? The very first line puts him "In the Shreve High football stadium." He is a participant! His poem knows there is something wrong with what he beholds, and yet it must also captivate him to some degree. Notice that the spectacle he witnesses is not merely terrible and violent but is also "suicidally beautiful." Those two words are the profound imaginative triumph of Wright's work here. They show how, in lyric (as in life, or at least my own), disparate and even contradictory impulses can exist simultaneously.

Perhaps I am simply clutching at justification for my TV-watching habits, seeking comfort in Whitman's famous "Do I contradict myself? Very well, I contradict myself. I am large, I contain multitudes." But I'm not large, and I know it. I suspect in plain truth that I willingly suspend my adult skepticism and even my ethical inquietude when I watch a great game of basketball or baseball that involves a Boston team. I see "my" players as heroes malgré moi. In fact I can even, if grudgingly, admire the prowess of players from opposing teams.

Even in my moment of hockey "greatness," I understand, I could never have dreamed of doing the things that I see on the screen; but to observe these extraordinary feats of physical skill and intelligence is still to recall that ancient, overwhelming, lit-from-within enthusiasm of the Hotchkiss game, a feeling that remains a sort of iconic moment in my soul.

But I need to finish this now. The NBA playoffs have begun, and my Celtics are taking on the uppity Atlanta Hawks in a matter of minutes.

CLOTHES

Fleda: Unruffled

WELL, YOU'D THINK THIS ONE would be MY subject. But I never had any clothes. That is how it felt. Oh, when I was a child, the first child, first grandchild, I was the darling of my grandparents' and my aunts' hearts. They crocheted, knitted, stitched, embroidered. There are boxes and boxes full of photos of me, wonder-child bedecked in sweaters, scarves, wool coats with fur trim, fur muff, delicate flowered sundresses and sunbonnets. Then I grew up.

My parents were getting along on my father's assistant professor's salary, with three, then four children, one of them seriously retarded and needing very expensive drugs. And neither of my parents thought of "managing" money. They talked and yelled and cried about "budgets," but nothing ever changed. At least once a year, one of the grandparents would be applied to for assistance, which would arrive, accompanied by the fury of my father in having to accept it. Well, enough of that. The fact is, I had at least one requisite new dress in the fall when school started, usually two, plus new shoes, usually courtesy of a grandparent. Care packages of clothes would arrive now and then, things picked out by my grandmother, never clothes I wanted to wear. Many of them were a terrible embarrassment, all wrong for what I felt was stylish in my crowd, but I was made to wear them anyway. They were new and they were "nice."

There was one sweater, white with appliqued flowers on it—a name brand and expensive. But the short sleeves had a tiny bit of a puff to them that felt dorky to me. And the flowers! Furthermore, my sister was given a matching one. A deadly move on my grandmother's part. I was made to wear the sweater to school. I may not remember this right, but in my memory, as soon as I felt I could get away with it, I deliberately held the sweater under hot water until the bright flowers on the applique faded onto the white sweater. "How can I wear it, now?" I asked. Did I really do that or just dream of it? I can't remember, but I am pretty sure that the fading happily happened. Of course my mother was somewhat careless about sorting clothes, so I may not have been the culprit.

Actually, after I got past the shorts-with-no-top age, I never had things I wanted to wear. I was furious when I was made to cover up with little halter tops, even before I had breasts. I was furious when I was made to wear dresses to school every day when I wanted to wear pants. Jeans were still in the future, but I would have invented them had I known how. I was most furious when I was made to wear a bra. I threw it across the room after one day in its miserable straightjacketing. I was furious when I had to wear stockings and garter belts and huge, full skirts with huge, full slips under them. I did not want to be a "lady," although I didn't particularly have an objection to being a girl.

Conversely, I longed to have ballet-slipper shoes, but I had flat feet and was forced to clump around in saddle oxfords or brown "Girl Scout" shoes.

Maybe I would have had fewer objections to girl clothes had I been able to buy the clothes many of my friends had—matching Bobbie Brooks sweater sets, straight and pleated wool skirts. The only days that I felt good about my clothes were the days the pep-club, called the "Peppers"—of which I was one—were required to wear their uniforms to school. We had white sweaters with a big purple B on the front, over a bulldog's face, and purple pleated skirts. I fit in. I was just fine.

I was asked to join a high school girls' sorority. Part of the initiation process was that two members had to come to your house and pick out an outfit from your closet that you were required to wear to school every day for a week. They usually picked outlandishly mismatched clothes, silly things. The two girls who came to my house looked through my closet while I stood aside, trembling with embarrassment. I had so few clothes and they were all so, well, not-quite-right. I could tell the girls were nonplussed. They did the worst thing possible: they felt sorry for me. They chose the nicest skirt and blouse they could find.

I always felt that part of the problem was me, that it was my fault I had no clothes. I was so headstrong: with my baby-sitting money, I bought some beautiful plaid wool fabric. I had this idea I'd make myself a skirt and vest. I cut it out. I cut it out wrong. I had no practice and no guidance. Did I slow down and ask a friend's mother for help? No. The awkward puzzle pieces I had cut would not go together properly. I stuffed them in a drawer, feeling wretched and guilty, and tried to forget.

Seething underneath the clothes issue for me was the tacit sense of the role women were supposed to play. The clothes were indicative. By the time I was seven, I had to put on that halter top. But the boys didn't. I had to wear dresses with ruffles, which made me feel decorated, ornamental, and as powerless as my mother. I hated ruffles and still do. This is not, as I said, a matter of wanting to be a boy. It is a matter of wanting to move freely and feel essential, just myself, an L.L. Bean sort of person.

I look at the models in the ads in the New York Times. They seem to combine, these days, a look of both power and glamor. At least that's what they apparently want to show: sleek tigresses, beautiful, furry, seething with power. But look into the eyes. It looks dead in there: the ads are pictures of women required to project tigresses. Women whose job is to sell clothes, who are desperate to hold their position in the world of high fashion, who will project anything you ask them to project.

Oh, really, I do like clothes. I always have loved the days when I've felt beautiful in my clothes. In the seventies, I had a pair of blue corduroy bell-bottoms and platform shoes that made me feel sharp and sexy. I bought one mini-skirt, which I thought was kind of cute, but I was teaching school and found that if I raised my arm to write on the blackboard, I exposed more of me than my students needed to see.

In those few years I taught high school, I made some of my own clothes (yes, I did!): pants and tops, as well as many curtains and pillow covers. I made a few cute outfits for my daughter, one little bell bottom jumper with big lady-bugs all over it, with a matching purse. She was five or six and looked very Mod. I liked sewing. I was not too bad at it. It was all-absorbing, meditative, and I could imagine I was saving money. Then when clothes got cheaper than fabric, I gave it up. Also, I had more and more things to do that seemed more important to me than sewing.

I attribute my ambivalent attitude toward clothes to two things: my early lack of money and my tomboyishness. The purchase of clothes was always accompanied by a great deal of angst when I was young. There was so little money that when I had any to spend, I was terrified I'd make a wrong choice. I often did. And had to live with it. If I'd used my own money, I knew that every dollar I spent equaled two hours' baby-sitting time. I would buy something, my stomach knotted up both from fear of making a mistake and fear of my father's yelling about the money spent. I grew cagey about the latter. I could fudge on how much something cost. I could say I had to have it for school for some obscure reason. I could say I'd used all or half my own money. Or something.

And then the tomboy-thing. I wanted to look beautiful, I wanted to look like the girls in my class I admired. But what made me happiest was climbing around creekbanks in pants (no jeans yet, remember) and an old flannel shirt, looking for crawdads. Those clothes were the ones I loved best.

I think about the sociology of clothes. In the fifties and on into the early sixties, the styles, the requirements in clothing for girls and boys were as separate as our psychology was thought to be. Girls had to wear dresses to school unless the temperature was below a certain degree, I can't remember what. But those days felt free as holidays, although we generally felt we must wear a skirt on top of the pants. When I was an undergraduate, girls were not allowed to wear pants on the University of Arkansas campus, except under a raincoat. And furthermore, they were not to wear them downtown. After all, they were "representing the University." All winter, all of my young life, my legs were freezing cold. Because I was a girl.

Boundaries were clear. Unlike now, when cast-off 50s dresses are worn with cowboy boots, tight torn jeans with diamonds and a sleek silk camisole, a tuxedo with tennis shoes. And too, when future anthologists—if there are any—look back on this era's poems, they'll see hybrid poems that pull in all manner of objects and thoughts and commercials and movies and music. Poems in received forms and free-verse poems, poems that announce that they're poems but look and read like prose. And prose poems. Soft boundaries between genres.

And self-conscious display of the making, the mechanics of the poem. The poet stepping in to say how it's going, this writing of a poem. Last weekend I attended a baby shower. The very-pregnant mother was wearing a long, form-fitting top and long skirt—very chic. It's fashionable to let the belly show, the stark progression of belly-growth, to be proud of it. When I was pregnant, maternity clothes were shapeless bags we buttoned over our midsection to hide the protrusion. We were only a generation or so from the time when pregnant women were expected to stay inside as they started "showing," as if any display of our sexual potency was shameful.

But even though now a woman can wear anything, really anything, she wishes and be acceptable on most occasions, somehow underneath, it feels to me as if that change hasn't netted as much as we'd like to think. The truth is, I see in the faces of some of those women in pillbox hats and blue suits on reruns of ancient game shows more maturity and more command of themselves and their environment than I see in the faces of many young women today, who seem uncertain of who they are and what they want to be. Those women in pillbox hats were fitting themselves into a role, true, but they knew they had responsibility for that role, for enacting it well and truthfully—being a good wife, a good mother, a good housekeeper. These were not the women on Mad Men. The ones I'm thinking of were the real ones.

I don't want to go back there, and couldn't if I did. Same with poetry. This is an incredibly exciting time for clothes and poetry, it seems to me. Exciting and necessarily unnerving. What we wear, what and how we write, is either demonstrating who we think we are, how we think the world is organized and what it all means, or it's demonstrating who we're supposed to be according to our culture's norms. Who can tell which is which? These days I wear jeans almost all the time. I'm an attractive woman for my age, but not a glamorous one, although I passionately admire my gorgeously dressed friends. The glamour-gene bypassed me. I have a friend, a writer, who said her goal in life is to make enough money with her writing to be able to get up every morning, her only decision being which pair of jeans to put on. Amen to that.

RE: CLOTHES

Syd: A Thin Disguise

Y ES, THE SUBJECT OF CLOTHES, particularly of whether we determine our sartorial looks on our own or some power in society does—well, it sets me to wondering once again about our cherished myth of individuality. Ask some suburban white boy clad in baggy pants, his hat on sideways, some monstrous chain slung from his neck what he's up to. He'll likely say something about being his own man, no matter that literal millions of kids his age worldwide have gotten themselves up in the same ludicrous fashion. Ditto tattoos: the time to sport one of those was when it might have started a bar fight, not when the toniest Upper East Side Manhattanite has his or hers.

But.

But when I was in mid-adolescence, not old enough to drive but close enough to ache for the chance, I must have read or heard Mark Twain's famous dictum, "Clothes make the man." I must also have failed to understand the humor of the great man's remark, never getting as far as the next sentence: "Naked people have little or no influence on society." Be all that as it may, the following is an account of how I was disabused, at least for the most part, of any notion that, by cannily attiring myself, I'd find influence and charm.

It's a story I myself can hardly believe, yet I'm the one who watched it unfold.

In the summer of my tenth grade year, I took a job I'd wish on nobody, one to make toll collection or highway flagging look positively stimulating. I can't remember the company that hired me, the interview process, or any of my colleagues save the straw boss, Goldie, who— ahead of his time, it seems—wore what we now call bling around his neck.

Goldie insisted on playing some elevator-music radio station loudly enough to foil conversation among his drones, though why he thought talk would be a distraction I can't imagine: the work was so reiterative that it required virtually no exercise of mind, only the most basic motor skills. Essentially, if you could metabolize, you could do it. We might as well have listened, as I would much have preferred, to R & B on the black-owned North Philly station, WDAS.

Even the late Etta James's raunchy rendition of "Roll With Me, Henry," so scandalous for its era, would scarcely have interfered with our tedious chore—making airplane maintenance manuals. I don't recall what the plane in question might have been: Goldie encouraged no curiosity on the job site. I hardly need mention that today's office technology existed at best in some mad scientist's dream back then. Our method of collating the manual was echt primitive: by the time we arrived, Goldie in his exalted post would have piled thirty or so pages in separate stacks around a banquet-sized table. We workers would slowly circle, picking up one page at a time until, at the final station, having assembled a complete set, we'd each place a bundle on the desk, behind which sat Goldie with his Brobdignagian stapler.

We proceeded clockwise for four hours, broke for a half-hour lunch, then—in some antediluvian gesture toward the OSHA of the future, meant, I suppose, to negate repetitive motion syndrome—we'd walk three and a half more counterclockwise. This was the one adjustment that demanded anything resembling concentration. We had now to put our pages on top of one another, not under. Though I can't picture his face as I write, I do recollect the firing of one hapless dolt who on his first day failed to make that adjustment. Goldie slammed his mammoth stapler down as a judge might his gavel, took two bucks from his pocket, handed them to the guy, and pointed, wordless and magisterial, at the door.

It was the usual muggy mid-Atlantic summer, the air thick enough to slice with a dinner plate and rife with the stink of the black cigars that Goldie smoked one after another. The atmosphere and the labor were trance-inducing, the lot of us staggering through our day like so many undead.

And yet, after two weeks it seemed adequate consolation to have money for a certain pair of pants. I'd had my eye on them from the moment I noticed them in a window hard by my streetcar stop. They closely resembled the pants I'd seen some local hero sport at the Sanatoga Speedway, a dirt stock car oval out in the countryside, which I prized above almost any place I knew. He'd been wearing them as he accepted a trophy in front of the grandstand—and he'd had a Jayne Mansfield-looking babe draped all over him.

A rather strange loneliness seems to pervade so many of the chapters I've written for this volume.

The pants were shockingly red, nay scarlet, their pleats deep enough to hide a magician's rabbit if need were. In short, they were garish, though I wouldn't of course have described them so back then, even if I'd known the adjective.

But in any case they'd be no more than a half of the costume I had in mind for myself. The summer before, I'd gone to California with my grandmother. Her only surviving son lived in the Berkeley hills, along with his wife and three of my first cousins. The male cousin, Ricky, had on several occasions sported what he called a gaucho shirt. I found it so fabulously cool that I talked my grandmother into buying its twin for me.

When I got back home, however, I discovered to my dismay that I really had no pants, casual or formal, to do the gaucho shirt justice. I wore my jeans—or dungarees, as my more bucolic friends called them—in the de rigueur manner of the age, their cuffs turned up five inches or so, pale inner fabric contrasting with the deep blue of the outer denim. When I stood before the mirror, the new shirt and the jeans seemed complementary with regard to color, but somehow they just didn't work as ensemble.

The gaucho shirt was almost navy at the top, but it gradually faded to paler blue and then paler as it descended, until at the waist it looked just shy of white. It also had a collar I found beyond merely cool: there was whale-bone or some synthetic facsimile sewn into it, and one could bend that bone to suit his personal taste. I recall straightening the collar horizontally, then pinching the ends straight down, so that my arrangement looked somewhat like a quick, side-to sketch of a cot, level plane with short legs at either end. It vaguely remembered what people, in honor of band leader and crooner Billy Eckstine, once called a "Mr. B collar."

I just knew right off that the bright red pants were what my outfit lacked, and I bought my pair right after my second Friday on the job, when the downtown stores had extended hours. I put my old jeans into a small duffel I'd brought along, and wore my new purchase right out of the dressing room. I'd carried the blue-on-blue shirt in the same bag, and, like Superman in his phone booth, I donned it inside the Horn and Hardhart men's room.

I'd hoped to feel like Superman too, the world at my command. But no.

I still felt, rather, like the slightly overweight, slightly shorter-than-average kid that in fact I was. I'd looked forward to seeing the Catholic girls who always boarded the streetcar late on Fridays, after something called *Sodality*, and who somehow seemed far more womanly than my WASP neighbors. They appeared to have real breasts, and I'd been titillated to observe several of them shamelessly smoking cigarettes at the trolley stop. These young women wore loud lipstick, and their parochial school uniforms, so far from seeming bland to me, struck me as strangely exotic and erotic. I'd prayed that one or two of these girls would at least give me the once-over.

But no.

Every Friday I'd also treat myself to an early-evening meal at the Grove Diner, very close to the end of the streetcar line, about half a mile uphill from my house. The Grove was also directly across the street from Streeper's drugstore, whose windows showed those bizarre, oversized vials, filled with mystery liquids of amber, indigo, mauve.

On this particular Friday, one of the windows also showed the plaster bust of a man wearing a black eye patch. And I got notions.

I'd always admired the male Hathaway shirt model in the newspaper and magazine ads, and now in some derangement I imagined that in fact the Hathaway man's eye patch was the real missing accouterment to my west coast shirt and my vivid trousers. I felt blessed that I'd kept enough money after my purchase (the precious pants turned out to be cheaply made, their seams unraveling after precious few wearings)—I had cash enough to buy the eye patch and still get my usual diner meal: a chicken salad sandwich with a tall glass of tomato juice.

I bought the eye patch from the puzzled clerk, ducked around the corner and put it on, then crossed the street to the Grove.

As I said at the outset, it seems beyond incredible now that I imagined an inch-square patch of cloth over one eye might serve as an actual disguise. Perhaps the eight-hour circuit of the table, along with inhalation of that foul smoke, had addled my brain. In any case, I wasn't able to leave things alone; even greater madness percolated in my mind.

The summer I describe was 1956. The Hungarian uprising was just around the corner; so too the Israeli invasion of Egypt. I couldn't know that, and I fear it wouldn't have mattered anyhow. I had personal urgencies to deal with. It appears that some details from a movie, fully two years old by the time I speak of, had lodged itself in my subconscious. As if bright red pants and flamboyant shirt and eye patch weren't enough, I decided to add the stiff-legged limp of John Wayne in The High and the Mighty. I'd like to claim that there was some continuity between my work on airplane maintenance and the airborne drama of that silly old flick, but I doubt I registered that.

I still couldn't stop myself: just as I pushed open the door to the diner, I fancied that I needed a further touch. So help me God, I opted for a French accent.

Louie the counterman, who had greeted me, surely, some scores of times in his tenure at the Grove, looked at my get-up with a bemused expression.

"Allo-bonjour," I chirped. "I weel have ze cheecken salad sandweech and a glass of ze tomato jooze."

Louie showed an odd restraint, which I mistook for his being deceived by my pretense. He started for the little kitchen window to relay my order, the very same order I'd placed with him so many times before.

I was as if possessed. I couldn't check myself: "By ze way, you can call me Frenchy," said I, pronouncing the last word Frawnshee.

It all finally proved too much even for the decently inclined Louie. He leaned into the window and shouted, "Hey, Gene! One chicken salad on white…for Frawnshee!" And then he let out the most humiliating laughter I've experienced, before or since. It was loud, slow and affected. Har Har Har Har Har. Other customers responded with their own versions.

I reached up, pulled off the eye patch, stuffed it into the breast pocket of my California shirt. To his credit, Louie simply allowed me, without comment or query, to resume my ordinary personality and diction. We had both been American League baseball fans, and now lamented the removal of the Athletics to Kansas City in the same year of *The High and the Mighty*. He asked me if I meant to go deer hunting at my uncle's farm come fall. He told me that Gene's wife was pregnant again; it would be their fifth child. And so on.

Then I walked home in the welcome cool that now dropped on the evening. For some reason, I remember watching two gray squirrels, either scrapping or playing high up in a tulip tree by the road, where the sun still painted the leaves. I stood and beheld them for as long as they kept at it, admiring their skill and speed as they danced branch to branch. I recall too that, rather than deeply downcast and depressed, I felt as though some weight had lifted from me.

Once I'd dropped that ridiculous disguise, as I've reported, Louie went about his usual small talk with me; he seemed in fact, and as always, rather to like me. The lesson I learned from that, alas, was too temporary. As I recollect this bizarre episode, it occurs to me how much of my life thereafter I still spent in trying to be something I wasn't and couldn't be. In this case it had been a leg-injured, faux French-lisping, one-eyed, loud clothes-wearing dude, but this merely constituted an extreme example.

Never again would I resort to so blatantly idiotic a posture, though when I consider certain charades I acted out among my academic colleagues and, far worse, my students in my first years as a college teacher, the lack of blatancy does not amount to lack of idiocy.

The forbearance of my grandmother, who took me to California, may have owed itself to her knowing that life itself is a better lecturer than any single human. She let me have my hideous shirt. The old woman had a saying that drove me crazy in my youth, but whose wisdom is as conspicuous now as those long-gone red trousers back then.

Too soon old, too late smart.

T.S. Eliot wrote in *Four Quartets* that humility is endless. Humility in my opinion is likewise the basis of human maturity, and human maturity the basis of poetry—or at least of the poetry that attracts and intrigues me. I never again believed that clothes would make the man; but I had a lot of sad crops to pick before I got as smart as I'll ever be, which meant I'd learn the virtue of accepting the things I couldn't change—including, especially, my inevitably humble self.

Children

Fleda—The Writer's Double Vision

THERE'S A PICTURE OF KELLY taken one Christmas. She's wearing the little bell-bottom overalls I made for her, green with big ladybugs all over. And a matching purse with a long rope strap. She's prissing around in it, very pleased. I have cut her hair in a kind of Dutch-boy, which I've always thought looked great on her. This is before she asked to have it long—even though it looked stringy that way—which I of course agreed to. My mother and grandmother would never let me have my hair my own way.

There's a picture of Scott sitting on the ground in his shorts. He's about three. We're camping on the White River, and he's been playing in the dirt. The sun is striking his golden curls. He is breathlessly delicate and beautiful, with his thin little body and his curls and his smile.

There's a picture of Scott and Kelly, at the kitchen table in front of a birthday cake I'd made. Kelly's fifteen, I think. She looks miserable, having to pose. Scott would be ten. He just looks bored. I was not a bad mom. I was not a good mom. I was the best mom I knew how to be.

I want to tell this to my children, what they can't remember:

I do not know how it was for you. All I can know is how it was for me, holding you, holding your small hand as we walked up the steep Ozark hills, and around Rush Drive. Both of you, as I fought the fog in my mind, the weight of fog, the way it presses down without leaving any evidence. I can imagine the stories in your heart: you heard our voices from your bed and you were scared. You heard the words tightened into fists, you heard the crying, you went to play with your friends as fast as possible in the morning, or you buried yourself in the beanbag chair in your pajamas, in front of cartoons until I made you get dressed.

There are many variations. I have not wanted to say any of this because it makes me sad. Syd has great memories of his children in the middle of the tumult of his marriage. I have few. I have a few poems, not many about you. Not that I wasn't holding you dear in my heart all that time. Not that I wasn't cheering you on. Just that I was simultaneously buckled down, turned inward, thinking how to survive. Part of the survival was getting degrees, working, writing.

Writing was survival in the complex ways it always is, I guess. Survival of my Self when I felt subsumed by my frighteningly terrible second marriage. Survival of my mind. And economic survival. Degree rhymes with free. Also, writing was a joy. Something happy, a phrase, a word, plucked perfectly when nothing else was.

It was as if I were keeping you secret in my heart to save you, which was crazy, because you needed me to be out there IN your lives. I didn't think what I was doing, I just did what came next, one thing after another. I married your father because I needed someone to hold me, to be alongside me, at least, in my loneliness. Then I began to grow up. Then the chain of events that sent us apart. I married your step-father barely a year later because I was reeling and naïve and he was handsome and smart. He was so much like my father I thought this time I could fix him, fix my father. Those are the excuses. My reasons.

Nobody in my family had ever gotten a divorce, much less two.

How must it be to have a writer-mother? A mother who's on the watch, whose eye is turned inward-outward, making a sense of out things that is not directly related to the swing being swung, the ball being thrown, the flower being picked. Who turns to pick you up and you can see her mind turning on its other track as well?

I can't know how it was with you. Here is how it was for me, which I tell you now not to rake through the sadness but to pull some of the threads of joy out into the light. The joy of your presence in my life.

I would have had you, Kelly, or someone like you, when I was eighteen, if I hadn't lost that child. And the next. The doctor gave me DES to prevent another miscarriage. Now we know what damage that can do to a girl-child in later life. I have held my breath all these years. All is well, thank God.

I was barely twenty when you were born. I wanted to have "natural childbirth," but there was no training for it. As soon as the pain got severe, I gave in to the drugs. No one seemed interested in helping me make it through, and your father was white-faced, holding my hand. The last thing I heard was "She's crowning" as the drugs took over. I missed it. I missed your birth.

We named you Kelly against your great-grandmother Simpich's protestations. "That's a boy's name," she said. She wanted us to at least spell it Kellie. Little did she, or we, know that soon there would be hundreds of Kellys in the world.

I was foggy with terror when we brought you home—the awful responsibility of you. No one was nursing babies then, but I wanted to nurse you. The hospital sent me home with no instructions for nursing and a case of formula, "just in case." When my milk was barely starting to come in, you were crying a lot, not getting much yet, and so I switched instantly to formula. In a couple of days, the milk would have settled in just fine, but I was afraid, with no help. I sterilized bottles and got to work. You broke out in a rash, face and bottom, from the change. My breasts burned and ached. Then we moved to Little Rock. Then you had colic and I tried to leave you in your crib, as instructed, while you screamed. More than not, I picked you up. I was a sleepless haze, rocking you until you were quiet and setting you in bed, slow motion, holding my breath, praying you'd stay asleep.

How is this different from any other mother's story of my generation? The difference is the writer, telling it. Seeing double, looking at it again, not sitting around the kitchen table, but indelibly, on the page.

I would sit in the sunlight for an hour, watching you wiggle. I would put you in your walker and watch you scoot. I held you in front of the mirror to show you how wonderful you were. You were my mirror-image. You were magic, growing and laughing. You were perfectly you, the you you've always been: edgy, alert, beautiful. I would push you around the neighborhood, full of you, showing you trees and leaves and birds. Tucking your sweater around you to keep off the wind.

Later, we would take walks up and down the blossoming hills, your hand in mine, picking flowers, talking about birds and sunshine. When I think of those times, what I remember most is your hand in mine, your fine pale hair blowing from under your scarf.

When you were born, Scott, my marriage was coming seriously unraveled behind my back, with only my depression showing, and that having no name. The rooms of our little house on Jackson Drive vibrated with tension, with unhappiness. But this time I nursed you just fine, drinking beer to get the milk going. You were a darling and cuddly child, snuggled against me in the dark. Later, you piled your bed with stuffed animals, making your whole world soft.

You were Lego-crazy. You had heaps and piles, and you would work and work, then call for me to come and see what you'd made, each intricate detail: cars and strange vehicles, buildings, planes. I would crouch and look in the windows, try opening the doors, push them around a track with you. You were in love with tracks, with little cars that swung around the corners without falling off. With little cars that had doors that opened, little trucks that would dump things. You were not in love with team sports, especially not baseball. You skipped your Little League's championship dinner and didn't even tell us about it. They brought your trophy to the door.

Your hair was so curly I would sit with you in the bathroom and blow-dry it for you, even when you were in middle school. You probably didn't tell anyone that. I felt I had to put you together, since you didn't care to do it yourself. You would have lived in your pajamas, your hair flailing around all over your head.

I'm not telling you anything you don't already know. Is that maddening, to have your life spread out on paper as if it were your mother's property? I mean only to affirm the solidity of a life that at the time felt hazy, unmoored. I am looking at your faces, both of you. I am seeing your struggling faces and not flinching. It is not easy. I am flinching. My love for you was my salvation and my punishment, and always my joy.

᳗

The rest they know because they were old enough to know. They learned to negotiate around their step-father by ignoring and by silence and by being gone from the house. Kelly was a cheerleader, runner-up to homecoming queen. She and her friends, all with family troubles, too, it turned out, depended on each other for what they couldn't get at home. Scott burrowed down into Dungeons & Dragons, his books, his elaborate miniature car tracks, Legos, and Kiss. He had his interestingly nerdy friends.

᳗

Kelly, wouldn't you know, is a therapist, the kind who helps people whose lives are falling apart. Well, that was her intention. She hasn't worked for ages: she's raising four children and making a strong, loving family. Scott's a computer programmer, or, rather, an executive consultant for IBM. He works mostly from home. He can stay in his pajamas all day if he wants.

Neither child is a writer, at least not in the way I'm a writer. Their lives contain only the double-vision of awareness, or of afterthought. How is it with their own children? Do they see in them yet the gaps they would have tried to fill if they had known? They've both known what it's like to fear for a child's life. They've both stood by a bedside and felt they would die with fear and sorrow. They've both come through, with their children. I suspect that their love for them is the same as mine, like a turbine roiling and pitching me forever out of balance. The grandchildren are all so different: Josh, focused and exacting, now studying at Brown, utterly devoted to learning everything he can. Zach, taking a gap-year before college, perfectly out-of-step, playing his music. Both Josh and Zach great ball players, great trumpet and sax players, great friends. Noah, luminous child, everyone's friend, hot-shot fisherman, great cook. Abby, fashion queen, dancer, queen bee. Jake, swimmer, reader beyond his years, analytical, sweet, but pulling back at his age. Samantha, hearing the whole world slightly askew, now 13 and free of her special classroom arrangement to help her hear through the ambient sounds, tense, writing her poems, hiking with Scott, her dad, her first, best love, at their Indian Princess outings. All of them from me, from what I was, what I meant, plus all the other hopes that entered along with me. Entering and passing through to the end, which will carry the residue of me, without knowing what.

When we're together, just the three of us, all adults, there is for me that feeling I remember from long ago, of circling our wagons without ever saying it. The three of us not "against" the world, more like inside the world, a self-sustaining system in which each of us knows the others, way beneath the surface. Each of us with our particular way of seeing and acting that balances the others', each of us knowing the flaws of the other in an almost joyous way. This is us, who we are.

I look in their adult faces: stoic, determined, loving. I see the long shadow that was cast before my time and cast again by me, and will be cast again. It is the shadow of imperfect love, the darkness left when we turn away and don't see. Not cruel, but oblivious. I didn't see. No matter what I wrote, how many poems, I didn't see that there was no time, that there was only that time. And this time, now.

We are all at the lake, at our cottage that was our cottage long before they were born. We are all together. We are sitting at the end of the dock on our ancient folding chairs. The kids splash us as they run past and jump in. Then Zach is out there on the stand-up paddleboard. Noah is rocking it to see how long Zach can stay on. Jake is circling in the small kayak. Sam and Abby are cold from swimming and are wrapped in beach towels on the dock. What are we talking about? Food, shampoo, weddings, books, movies—the usual ramble, sometimes intense, sometimes delicately sidestepping, sometimes just keeping the words going. We are a family.

↔

"Home is the place where, when you go there, they have to take you in," wrote Frost. We're held to each other by our genes, by our memory of hurt, of joy—it doesn't matter which, in a way. We arrive at the cottage so glad to see each other that we hardly know how to express it. I keep rubbing Scott's back or ruffling his shorter but still wildly curly hair. I touch Kelly more gently and with more caution. Each of us survives in our own way. In the photo—all of us on the cottage porch—we are a mass of arms and legs and smiles. Abby has lost a big front tooth. I tell her she looks like Alfred E. Newman. She has no idea who that is.

RE: CHILDREN

Syd: What's Normal, What's Better?

IS IT HARD-WIRED INTO ALL of us, mothers and fathers alike, the heartache? I'm not sure, but Fleda, you have just said a mouthful on the subject. Any decent parent knows what it is to be conscious of his or her offspring in a way that is like no other consciousness; I can't say precisely how, and I surely wouldn't speak on behalf of the world's vast array of poets, but it seems inevitable that such consciousness would figure profoundly into one's poetry, whether or not the poet knows it at any given time.

I haven't asked you if you share it, but as for me, I begin by noticing in myself a certain undeniable bigotry: as father to five, I lend a good deal less credence to the opinions and observations of people who have no children at all than I do to parents. I even apply this unfair predisposition, though far less strenuously, to those with single children.

Yes, I'm unfair to several very good friends who are childless, for starters: I think especially of one couple, more than dear to me, but married, still blissfully after many years together, when the woman partner was beyond child-bearing age. (It is telling, at least to me, that they make nonpareil uncle and aunt; I always find some way to get my cherished ones off the hook, you see.)

Perhaps I'm unfair, period. And yet for one thing, however blessed as father I've been by my children's health and well-being, I know what it is to imagine catastrophe: worry for one's offspring is qualitatively different from any other sort of anxiety. You can't know it if you haven't been there.

Why, however, should these musings on raising children begin with notes on fear and misery? If I had to guess, I'd say it's because I believe every parent meditates on his or her missteps, on how—despite having received no training, after all, for so crucial a job—he or she could have done something to prevent even the slightest unhappiness in his or her child. My question for me, though, is whether I dwell on these things more than most parents do.

Not that I'll ever forget the un-slight ways in which I should have tried to avert the children's larger agonies, especially those of my firstborn, now 41, but only eight when I divorced his mother, ten when I married his stepmother. I'm pretty sure I couldn't have kept that first marriage alive, though not for any fault in my wife. I'd never unwish the marriage, given the wondrous children who came of it eventually, but I surely married too young, less with respect to years (even if 23 now does seem to me a perilous time to take such a step) than to maturity. How little I knew of the world and human relations! For example, I was engaged to marry that noble and generous woman in June of 1966. Earlier in the same year—February, to be exact—my 56-year-old father had dropped dead of a coronary. My mother quite rightly liked my fiancée, and I simply repressed any doubts, of which I felt more than a few, about my readiness to wed, persuading myself that I couldn't in good conscience lay yet another shock on my reeling mother so soon.

Besides, I figured, this being the hang-loose sixties, I could always get divorced.

Guess what? It wasn't that easy. Not until after sixteen years and a son and a daughter did my first wife and I part ways.

That was more than three decades ago. I've been with the woman I later married for almost this whole span. I was blessed to have the children of the first marriage under my roof at least half the time until they grew and left. They and the younger three blended beautifully, calling each other brother or sister as if they all shared the same blood; more and more, they offer me the greatest riches of existence. Whatever early adjustments there were, they are also close to their stepmother, and their own kids think of her as one of their grandmothers.

You'd think such good fortune would help me forget how much sadness attended their upbringings.

Or did it?

In some measure, of course, yes. But do I inflate my part in the sorrow? Again, I feel clueless. I am constitutionally inclined, as I know, to blame all their unhappinness—indeed, at times, any unhappiness I behold, past or present—on my own contribution to it. It remains hard nonetheless to excuse, let alone forgive my own alcoholism, say, even if I buy its diagnosis as a disease. I know it affected my children, especially the older ones, though again, I have since been graced by recovery, as that poor mother never was.

Is such epical self-blame "normal" to parenthood? I can't even say, though I fear I must surmise the role of that old monster egoism in all this, however strenuously I've tried to slay it. How can I think my role so central, really, to anything, if not for ego?

Whatever the case, I've never so much as discussed the matter with dear friends, and I have a great number, who are fathers themselves. Perhaps, having written this, I will, but until I know better, I'll go on asking why I can't batten more firmly onto the undeniable joys I have shared with my kids, above all in these later years, and especially since becoming a grandparent four times over?

Why, more puzzlingly, do I tend, even when recalling the joys, somehow to find an underlying pathos?

My oldest son Creston has gained rightful fame as a custom guitar-maker; he is also author of *Wild Punch,* the best short fiction about our home ground that I know. But back when he was five or six, he wanted to be another sort of artist. The boy asked me every evening to give him a drawing lesson, not that I had any remarkable aptitude myself. (His adult skill as an occasional dabbler became extraordinary; indeed, his skills are legion.)

For over a year, the only thing he chose nightly to render was an Army jeep. It was at that time too that he learned to whistle between his teeth, so that when I yet feel the shin-high chill of winter in our drafty little kitchen, it is broken by jets of whistling, some of those nights so arctic that the notes issue as small clouds. But neither cold nor another thing distracts him. The tires. Then the fenders. The side panels. The windshield. The steering wheel. The stub of exhaust pipe under the tailgate. The whole process, for all my shivering there, is a pleasure to recall. And it fills me with lamentation.

You will say that in this and all the other cases I'll remember, I'm merely mourning the children's passage out of innocence. You will be right, of course, but there's something else there too, something just beyond my articulation. Again, it's the sense that in those moments I should somehow have done the drawing lesson, and so many other things, better, more generously. I was there, all right; but I should have been more so.

I consider that oldest son, father now to a five-year-old daughter and a two-year-old son himself, each a brilliant beacon in my life; I watch his younger sister, mother to boy-and-girl twins about to turn three—another pair of dazzling lights. I see what gifted parents both are, and wonder whether a single element of their gifts was passed along by their father. I generally conclude that none does, that their manner derives principally from a magnanimous mother.

I also wonder if, when their own children are grown and gone, they will sit and brood like me on certain omissions, of which at day's end every parent must be more or less guilty? I mean, I genuinely do wonder that. To repeat, I can't seem to evaluate how "normal" I am.

Erika, the twins' mother, once asked me to make her a certain toy. I remember being a bit irked, not at the request but, compared to virtually every other Lea male in prior generations and in my children's, at my unhandiness with tools. Still I soldiered downcellar and there cobbled together the crudest imaginable facsimile of an airplane, which was what the daughter had wanted. Making body, tail and wings, however rough, was as far as I could go: I didn't even contemplate a propeller.

I brought the contraption upstairs, hiding it behind my back, less by way of presenting a surprise than of concealing for as long as possible my own shameful ineptitude. And I will never forget my daughter's sudden, audible inhalation, the look of wonder in her eyes, the grateful embrace she gave me.

I felt awful. I still feel awful. I should have made something better.

The next in line is Jordan, a strapping fellow, among the few men I know who make me, no inconsiderable physical figure, feel entirely tiny. He resembles an NFL lineman minus the blab. But he's a prince, who a few months back married a princess whom his parents adore. For all his size, I remember his mother's pride, and my own, at hearing a teacher describe Jordan as the classroom peacemaker, an endowment he has carried into adulthood. Accomplished in all manner of ways, he's now a snowboard instructor and a wilderness guide for troubled kids, and he's back in Vermont, thank God, after five years in Alaska.

As a boy, Jordan once did. . .something. I can't even remember what. Saxophone recital? Basketball game? No matter. All I summon from that moment is his asking me, quietly and with patent self-doubt, "Did I do a good job?" I forget how I responded, and yet, though I'm sure I praised him, I instinctively assume, yes, that I should have praised him better.

The following child, Catherine, showed an early interest in poetry and, if she chooses to go after it for fair, will in time write so well that I'll be largely remembered, if at all, not as author myself but as Catherine Lea's father. (Fine by me, incidentally.) As I drove her to elementary school, we used to play what we called the Slant Rhyme Game. One of us would start, for example, by saying road. The other would then say something like read, and then did, and then rude, and so on, the object being to get back to the first word by the time we pulled into the schoolyard, but not a minute before.

How bright, how inventive she was, and still is. How much finer a game I should have invented for bringing out that fine genius.

Then came the youngest, my namesake daughter, who is—along with being an extraordinary poet herself and a divinely kick-ass singer—one of the funniest persons I know, if not the funniest. (When I was lately made state poet of Vermont, for instance, she told me the title was pronounced "poet low-rate.") Pretty as she is, merely to see her is to start laughing; it's uncanny.

With Sydney I played a different game on the way to school, the Animal Game, whose aim was for each player to spot an animal before the other did. To do so was to earn a point, though we did have special rules for special sightings: an eagle, say, or a moose, which would be worth five points, not one; and nothing was awarded for seeing common things like crows or ravens or songbirds.

Naturally, whoever had called out the names of the most creatures on arrival was the winner. I took a variety of ways to school, sometimes the Interstate, sometimes New Hampshire route ten on the east shore of the Connecticut River, sometimes Vermont route five on the west, trying to avoid patterns whereby she'd be primed to find that mule, for example, who liked to hide in the shadows of the Scotts' barn. No matter my strategies, however, I almost never won, largely, I'd want to protest, because I had to keep my eyes on the road, at least most of the time. But Lord, she was and is a sharp one!

As I've been from her infancy, I'm crazy about that kid, now 21, sophisticated and a whole lot wiser than I at twice her age. She deserved something of higher quality than that silly contest on our countless rides.

This ongoing pathos: it shouldn't, to wit, attend my experience last week during a visit with the youngest grandchild. Arthur grabbed a blue truck, shaking it vigorously, then running it up and down my leg like a shearsman harvesting wool, then, a ball of high laughter, reaching up with both arms to be lifted and hugged goodbye.

Sorrow and regret should play no part in that moment, but they do. I ought to be a better lifter, maybe. Maybe a better hugger.

God damn it, I'm close to weeping as I write.

My children are adults. They have each been around the block in a variety of ways. In fact, their adventurousness—one, for a single example, taking her junior year abroad not in Paris or London or Madrid, as I might have given the chance, but in Havana—makes the provincialism of my own school and college years all the more glaring. My sons' and daughters' precocious and far-ranging experience allows them to read character unusually well. Hence they know how given I am to self-laceration and even, on occasion, though less and less for some reason as grandfatherhood becomes an exalting habit, how given to despondency.

I don't think, though, they can understand that inclination in their father.

How could they, when he can't himself?

BECOMING A POET

Fleda: Miracles

I SUPPOSE AT THE MOST MUNDANE, I became a poet when the poet-part of how I see myself began to take precedence over other parts, when I had a few good publications and saw that if I continued to write poems, there might be a future for me. But "being a poet" feels to me more a condition than a vocation. It's not even about loving words. "How did you learn to love words?" is an easier question to answer. I learned to love words because my father loves words. He's 94 now and he writes me one or two 3-5 page letters a week, banged out single-spaced on his old manual typewriter, all about the economy, religion, how he's managed to fix his clock, his constipation, whatever randomly occurs to him, in no particular order. He loves to recite poems: "The Highwayman," "Jabberwocky," "Invictus," "The Boy Stood on the Burning Deck," and on and on—he belonged to a choral poetry-recitation group in high school, back when the ability to say poems aloud was part of what it meant to be cultured. He loves to look up words: the dictionary was the most-used book in our house, pulled out at least twice a day.

But as I said, that's the easy question. I could have become a journalist, an essayist, a novelist, or a banker, I guess, with the same credentials. I think when the love of words strikes the longing of the heart for—shall I call it God?—poetry is the result. When I say God, I mean the insatiable longing to see more, to know the truth of things, to see through, to love the ordinary details so much that they crack open and let us in on their secrets. All that is fancy language and I don't know what it means. All I know is that when I write poems, I am after a holy mystery that I know I can only touch the hem of.

So I need to start over with my self-analysis, with my young spirit, in a pew in the large First Christian Church in Columbia, Missouri, and then its replica in miniature in Fayetteville, Arkansas, my young spirit held breathless by the language of the King James Bible, words that had climbed to the highest rung in their attempt to say what couldn't be said, what could only be revealed in song and stories lifted toward the heavens. It is that—what can't be said—that I fell in love with. I mean seriously in love, romantically in love, passionately in love. I have never gotten over it.

The first poem I remember writing, I was in the sixth grade. My father and I rewrote ""Twas the Night Before Christmas," beginning "'Twas the night before Christmas/ and all through the house,/ not a creature was stirring,/ not even a louse." I suspect this poem was almost entirely my father's invention, but I claimed it since he was saying it and I was writing it down. I probably did think of some of it.

In Junior High, I know I wrote some poems I can't remember and no longer have. I was more occupied with survival in the world of my peers, with my survival in life in general. That went on for, oh, the next twenty years or so. However, poems did get written during that time. In high school we were given a choice in English class of writing an essay or a poem. I chose poem. I think I still have that one somewhere. It was sweet and had a grandmother's rocking chair in it. I got an A.

After toying with Biology and Psychology and discovering the math and science involved in obtaining degrees in either of those fields, I became an English major, which was what my entire being had always intended. I took the only undergraduate creative writing course offered at the University of Arkansas. In that class, taught by a woman who smoked English Ovals and made me long to emulate her arty coolness, we were asked to write poems and short stories. I poured out the poems and labored through the stories. But the stories were pretty good for a first try. "How did you know to write this?" she wrote on one story about a traveling salesman, a Willy Loman character, before I'd read "Death of a Salesman." I don't know. I just wrote it because I heard his loneliness and sadness. With my sheaf of poems typed onto thin erasable bond, I was runner-up for the poetry award on Honors Day.

At the end of that spring, my husband graduated and took a job in Kansas City. I was pregnant. Almost immediately I started taking correspondence courses, and when we moved back almost two years later (my husband changed jobs because we wanted to be in Fayetteville), I re-enrolled and picked up where I'd left off. When I finished my degree, I immediately started taking graduate courses (I was pregnant with Scott by this time), and collected nine credits by the time I was hired to teach high school in Springdale, just up the road from us.

Poetry seems to circle those of us who write it like a large bird, coming in closer and closer until we finally admit we're stuck with it forever. During those five years of teaching high school, I wrote poems when my students were reading in class. That is, when I wasn't grading huge stacks of papers. My life felt like hell, pretty much. My marriage was falling apart and I found it utterly exhausting to try to convince rural students to care about standard English, *Moby Dick, Leaves of Grass, The Scarlet Letter,* or even novels written specifically for contemporary young people. I loved many of my students and greatly admired many of my co-teachers. I was a good teacher. But after the second year, I knew I had to get out or wither up.

I've never forgotten, though, my students' hunger for what's real. I hear them, I see them, their eyes peeled for the words, the objects, of their world, their pleasure in seeing those objects and that language raised up in recognition of the actual life we live together. I saw what poetry could mean to them.

I remarried, resigned my job, and went back to graduate school. Arkansas had a top-notch MFA program—there were splendid student writers roaming Kimpel Hall: Leon Stokesbury, Frank Stanford, Barry Hannah, Jack Butler (yeah, all men, I think). But I wanted the Ph.D. instead. It felt, frankly, like a more important degree, more serious. Besides, I would be more likely to get a job with the Ph.D. Besides that, my father had never finished his dissertation, and, wouldn't you know, it felt AS IF that task was out there for me to finish. Furthermore, I didn't trust myself to enter that world where everyone seemed more cool than I was. I couldn't even fake that writerly swagger in the hallways. Also, I knew how much reading I needed to do, how much discipline I needed.

I wrote a dissertation on the novels of William Dean Howells—a most unpoetic subject. Howells, a grand arbiter of literary taste as well as a respected novelist, reminded me of my Granddaddy Simpich—solid and secure.

Also, my best teachers were in American literature. A paper I wrote on Twain's *Mysterious Stranger* manuscripts won me the best graduate student paper award. I would have chosen to write my dissertation on the American short stories of D. H. Lawrence, but my new husband was writing his on Lawrence, and we didn't think we could both get jobs in the same field. Oh, I should mention that when I quickly, disastrously, fell in love with him, this gorgeous, sexy Lawrence scholar, I wrote him dozens of love poems, all of which he smiled indulgently at and thanked me for.

It was while I was writing my dissertation that the poems got better. I think the tedious work of typing, day by day, long passages of pedestrian prose, of doing research, of working from notes, circling and counting images in chapter after chapter (yes, God help me, I did an image study), drove me deeper into poetry.

I think what it was like, then. I would write longhand, then type—I was a poor typist—the poem. I would think of a revision as soon as I'd typed it. I would type a revised line, cut it out and paste it over the old one. By the time I was satisfied, the poor thing was a ragged heap of cut-and-pastes. I would type a final version. I would make a mistake. I would type it again.

I didn't know where to send things. There was no internet. Poems were accepted and printed in little magazines that I wish I'd never sent to, ones with flowers surrounding awful little poems on virtually mimeographed pages. But I hit the jackpot a few times, too, enough to show me what I might be able to do. *The Kenyon Review* took a poem, *Southern Humanities Review*, and *Cedar Rock*, a newspaper-style magazine in Florida, printed three poems and my photo, all of which filled the second page. On the front page was Diane Wakoski!

During this time, I put together several annotated bibliographies and wrote several literary essays, hoping to build credentials toward a real job (which I eventually got). I would wander the stacks of the library with briefcase and note cards, being what I thought a real scholar should be: contained, musty, focused. No, being a person playing a role and playing it pretty well, considering that I had to pretend to care about the bibliographies. It was a role I would have kept on playing, I suppose, if no one had wanted my poems.

Eventually I had enough poems to think of a book. Again, I had no idea where to send it and no friends in the poetry world to tell me. I had become friends with Jeanne Murray Walker, whose first book of poems had just come out from Cleveland State. She told me how she had queried all over; I prepared dozens of letters to every press I could find, asking if and when they accepted poetry manuscripts. I forgot to include an SASE! Many generous editors wrote back anyway, some of them scolding me for that omission while answering my question.

I don't remember how many presses I sent to that first time. Not many. I had had a few rejections when the editor at Purdue University Press called me. They liked my manuscript, "Fishing With Blood," a lot. They were going to take it to the editorial board, but she wondered if I might want to change the title, since it felt a bit off-putting. Oh yes, I would change my name, my religion, my nationality, and my race if needed. I said I'd think about a new title, but I called her back later to say I could not come up with a better one, so we agreed that I'd write an explanation for the name on the back cover.

Back cover! A miracle.

Second miracle: the book won the *Great Lakes New Writers Award,* accompanied by an invitation to read at eleven schools in the Great Lakes area. I had read my poems in public only a few times to this point. The first time, I had diarrhea all day before the reading.

This is the point when the lights get pinkish and dim and you're to understand that from here on it was pretty much wine and roses.

The thing about a second book is that the first does feel like a miracle, and miracles are doled out to most of us only, say, once a lifetime. I didn't believe in a second book. Even though Purdue automatically put my second manuscript into their top few, the judge didn't choose me. I sent and sent to other presses and it was rejected and rejected. But the next year, Gerald Stern did pick it, thank God. Five years between book one and book two.

Sufficient to say, each book and each poem has been starting from scratch. I am always afraid the last poem was a miracle that can never be repeated, and indeed, it can never be repeated. The next one has to be pulled from thin air. There must be a combination of utter humility and faith in what surely is available in me somehow, to do the work.

I am sure that a poem can only be as capacious as the person who writes it. The older I get, the more there is in me to use, the richer the poems seem to be. That gives me great pleasure. I honor and revere poetry. I feel that somehow I have grown into being its priest. Shelley said that "poets are the unacknowledged legislators of mankind," and I understand that, more and more. We think our rational, surface minds are in charge, but all the while the unseen rivers are driving us in one direction or the other. Poetry can, at its best, open the channels so that the rivers can be "seen" in some way. Their course can be changed. Or they can be widened.

In the early days, I met Donald Hall, who invited me to send him poems. I had been doing that for a while when Fishing With Blood was accepted. I wrote to him, wild with joy. He wrote back with congratulations, but added, "Remember that the poem is the thing. You can win prizes, you can win the Nobel Prize, for that matter, and always want more. If you set your sights on wanting the next thing, your poems will suffer. Pay attention to the poems only."

Actually, there's no choice. Every poem insists on full attention. I've spent—what?—half my life sitting in front of the blank page with both terror and joy.

re: Becoming a Poet

Syd: A Way of Knowing

WHO KNEW I'D CHOOSE POETRY as my prime mode of knowing the world? Not I.

It's true that as a high school punk, despite my significant enthusiasm for football and my wild one for hockey, despite my commonplace tough-guy posturing, practiced by so many of us guys at that stage of life, I liked to think of myself as a bit arty too. I was a musician. I even thought I drew pretty well. I was a big cheese in the dramatic club, as a senior playing Oedipus in the eponymous play (a lisping king, who at the outset had to address "generationth of the living in the land of Thebeth").

But I don't remember writing many poems, save the sort that any person may have written, and that any person hopes have long since utterly biodegraded: rants about breaking up with a girlfriend, just for a trite example.

I was also a pretty good student. Indeed, had it not been for what would now be diagnosed as a mathematical learning disability, my grades would have been of the very highest. My truest proficiency was foreign languages, a gift nourished by the best instructor I ever had at any level, the late Ted Wright, who taught French. I began to speak the tongue pretty quickly, and I recall how strange it was that the words and the grammar often seemed to be granted me by some power outside myself.

It's a feeling I would come to recall, if not as often as I could wish, when I composed a poem successful in my own eyes.

It's at once simple and weird: words and phrases, whatever the language, simply enchant me, seduce me, especially if I hear them. Things spoken in my presence, if they have a particular, inexplicable resonance, will lodge themselves in my mind for decades. For example, I lately remembered a friend's describing the death of his farmer uncle, who fell dead in his tracks while shutting the tailgate of his truck on a calf bound for the abattoir. I heard that description over forty years ago. I wrote the poem last week.

Like my exemplar Robert Frost, I want my poems to have something of the ring of actual talk in them. But that's to get ahead of myself. The college I chose had no writing courses as we know them in our era of rampant MFAism. But somehow, on my own, I started to feel an itch to write, which I did, my only audience, really, being my roommates, who tended to think I was pretty good. I limited myself to short fiction, and I wrote a lot of it in those four years; it seemed to keep me balanced somehow, while everything else was doing just the opposite.

Ultimately, of course, graduation loomed, and I had to figure out what I might do. Yale had accepted me as a grad student in French, but much as I loved the language and the literature, something in me recoiled from living as a kind of literary expatriate. I never imagined applying to a place like Iowa, though quantitatively, my portfolio would have permitted me to. (Who knows about the quality?) I had barely even heard of any of the few MFA programs that existed in those days. I never dreamed, either, of being a writer. I thought that professional writing was something other people did; there was some secret to it, and no one had shared it with me.

I did not want to go to Vietnam, as one roommate did, becoming one of the earliest casualties of that wrong-headed adventure. And so, because schoolteachers were exempt from the draft at that time, I elected to go back to my own private high school, having no credentials to teach in a public one.

I taught French and English, and came to understand how Ted Wright managed to be so inspired and inspiring a teacher. He simply committed himself to that end every minute of the day right through the evening's class preparation. No one messed with Ted: he was a big, muscular guy, the football coach, a former semi-pro pitcher. At a mere 21, I didn't have that sort of gravitas, and I devoted a lot of time to quashing the same sort of ill discipline I'd imposed on all my other teachers, now my forgiving colleagues, just a few years before.

Top quality high school teachers are, to my mind, the heroes of American education. They deserve to be paid a lot more, and college teachers (especially those at the sorts of "prestige" institutions where I myself have taught) a good deal less. To say it tersely, even after one year in a pretty cushy job at that level, I concluded there wasn't enough money in anyone's bank to keep me at it. Too hard, too demanding, too much time just being present.

So I did go to grad school after all, not in French, but not in English either. I did comparative literature, wanting to use my languages while I focused on fiction and poetry as fields of study. I was too naïve to know that comparative literature was just then leading that study in the "theoretical" direction that has made it unappealing to me and apparently—to judge from the shocking shrinkage in literature majors at the majority of colleges—to most students.

Not that my dabbling in theory didn't have its heady moments. I particularly recall a fabulous seminar on European Romanticism, presided over by the second best of my many teachers, Geoffrey Hartman. And yet Geoffrey became, quite unintentionally, a bit of a villain in my history. I had settled on a perfectly conventional dissertation topic, though I can't even remember what; he persuaded me, however, to expand one of my seminar papers, an examination of several supernaturalist authors of the nineteenth century, most of them deservedly forgotten. Unlike my other choice, he averred, this would be "a real contribution."

Contribution? What about nightmare? To indicate how sheep-like I'd been in acceding to my professor's suggestion, most of my texts were written in German, the one major western European language I didn't really know at all, which meant that I was forevermore rifling through the stacks for translations from the original into French or Spanish, few being available in my native tongue.

Good Lord. . .

Before long I took a job at Dartmouth, without, however, having finished that accursed dissertation. Indeed, it would take me more than four years to do so.

There were no writing courses at Dartmouth in those days, any more than there had been at Yale when I was there. But there had been a fair amount of clamor from students for that lack to be remedied. The result, in my second year, was English 70, an omnium-gatherum offering in which students could write fiction, poetry, drama, personal essays, what have you?

The heavies of the department, many of them good people and true, to be sure, were exclusively male—women adjuncts were referred to as "lady lecturers"!—and white and old, and at least marginally Christian. (These descriptives fit me better as I write this than they fit the people in question then; but such, in my late twenties, was my regard for them, one and all.) They assigned English 70 to me, of all people.

This was meant, though, as an act of kindness. Since in the eyes of those senior colleagues, such a course was not a "real" one at all, not the kind that demanded any genuine thought or preparation, I would have more time to complete my burdensome dissertation.

And yet a strange thing happened—or perhaps not so strange. In teaching that course, ineptly, I'm sure, given my utter lack of credentials, I found that old itch returning. It had been suppressed for at least half a decade, but now I began to write again myself.

I began, though, to write poetry. Why? Well, pardon a detour to something very relevant: my family has a relation to a remote part of Maine that goes back generations now; my brother and sisters collectively own our clan's cabin there. My time in the neighborhood had exposed me to certain notable characters, ones who would be 120 or so if they lived still. These were men and women whose early lives had preceded the advent of power tools, so that the male lumberjacks had cut millions of board feet by hand. And to call the females "housewives" would be downright laughable: they were stunningly hardworking people, who quite literally kept the home fires burning, who cooked in wood-fired ovens, who slaughtered chickens, skinned game, cleaned fish and did whatever else was called for to sustain a homestead.

Because they had no electricity, they had no radio either, let alone the great drug television. No, they had to make their own amusement, and the result was that, man and woman alike, they were fabulous raconteurs. Their magical turns of phrase ring in my head every day: some get into my conversation, a lot into my poems.

It seemed inevitable that, when I moved for my job to another part of northern New England, I sought out their Vermont and New Hampshire counterparts, who were equally eloquent, grammar and syntax be damned. And even at my young age, I somehow recognized mine was the last generation that would have known these precious souls.

I wanted to get their voices onto the page.

And yet I knew I was no genius. I wasn't Mark Twain or Willa Cather. I couldn't resort to dialect without on the one hand sounding condescending, which was the opposite of how I felt, or simply sounding "off," or both. I came to the conclusion, rightly or wrongly, that if I used poetry to tell their stories—or rather to tell stories suggested by their stories—I might capture the rhythms and cadences of that old-time, entrancing speech without having to imitate it.

My earliest poems, consequently, were in the main quite specifically narrative ones. And although I have drifted away from overt story-telling in my verse, I have never quit believing in certain conventional narrative values: if plot remains implicit, still I want my reader to know who's talking to whom, and where and why. Character, setting and dialogue: why should we poets have ceded these endowments so readily to the fiction writers?

To this day, and I am old enough now to be indifferent about what the Smart People think, I want my reader to know some literal truths when he or she encounters a poem of mine. I want to make that reader aware of who the characters are, perhaps especially the character named I. Readers, I hope, will be my allies: I'm grateful to them, and feel I owe them a welcome. They shouldn't be taxed by figuring out the plain facts of the matter.

One of the department elders I mentioned a short time ago—a man whom I greatly liked from those days up to his fairly recent death—was chairman at a critical juncture. He approached me one day and said, "People are starting to regard you pretty favorably around here, but you know the saying, publish or perish. I'm glad it didn't apply when I was your age, but without some scholarship in print nowadays, you have very little chance of tenure."

Well, then! I liked where I lived. I particularly liked the landscape and that access to the old story-tellers, and since in those days one did not have to publish a book but rather a few articles to pass the publish-or-perish test, I thought, okay, I'll just take a chapter or two from my dissertation (a screed incomprehensible even to its author) and try to stick them somewhere."

Mind you, I had gotten lucky with my poetry pretty quickly. I'd put poems in *The New Yorker,* the *Atlantic, The New Republic* and a slew of high-end lit magazines. But however different things are now at Dartmouth, in those days publishing poetry was not "real" publishing; that my first collection was under contract cut no ice.

I took the dissertation over to my library carrel, opened it up, and felt what I sometimes have upon looking over a shear precipice. My head spun, my stomach knotted, and I uttered aloud, despite the fact that I was in my thirties: "This is not what I want to do when I grow up." I closed that dusted-over tome, vowing that I would go on writing poetry and let the chips fall where they would.

I did not of course get tenure, but was fortunate enough as almost immediately to be hired by Middlebury College, where the tradition of writer-professors had been fairly long established.

I now ponder that cri de coeur of mine, and I wonder why scholarship should not have appealed to me as something to do as an adult; why it couldn't draw me more than it did or does. Understand, after all: nothing I say here is intended as an attack on scholarship. The contrary. I have benefitted enormously from other people's labor in scholarly endeavor. It's only that it isn't for me.

Or not to the exclusion of other things. Oh, I have done my share of more or less scholarly articles since, selected ones even appearing in book format, and have even enjoyed doing them. But something always seems missing when I finish. It's the missing something that's provided by so-called creative writing, especially the writing of lyric, however I must struggle here and elsewhere to name that element.

For me, poetry is another mode of knowing the world, one that is different from the either/or, syllogistic mode whereby people (myself included) generally conduct their business. It is an approach largely divorced from either/or, is in fact one better described, the way Carl Jung did human psychology, as a matter of either/and/or—which is to say that it enables the writer (and ideally the reader) to see and feel from multiple angles simultaneously.

It is this quality, I believe, that John Keats famously called Negative Capability: the capability "of being in uncertainties, Mysteries, doubts, without any irritable reaching after fact & reason." Any number of perceptions, emotions, thoughts, and so on can exist in a poem at the same time, including ones that are evidently contradictory of one another. And so poetry's path to knowledge, more nearly than any other, represents the path my mind seems to follow.

And of course there is again the matter of language. All those voices, old and new, anglophone and otherwise, that reverberate in my skull and, more importantly, in my heart. To abandon myself to what I called their rhythms and cadences, to let the words and phrases, as it were, bear me along like a tide to such enlightenment as I'll ever have—that feels, if you'll allow me, like a self-abandonment to something divine, and not just slightly.

POLITICS

Syd: The Inviolable Voice

DEAR, EXCELLENT FLEDA. To read your new chapter was to feel all manner of rabbits scooting into the underbrush—and, at least for the moment, to stand here dumfounded as to which I might pursue. In a time such as ours, after all, one would have to be plain obtuse not to agonize over what seem the world's manifold lunacies, to ponder how our art might help move us toward something better, and even –as we have discussed in private– now and again to wonder why the hell bother anyhow with so widely ignored a practice as the poetic?

Your thoughts got me thinking back on a conference that I attended, as I do annually, in beautiful Bled, Slovenia, a P.E.N. affair at which I tend to be the sole American among a group of largely central and eastern European intellectuals. One of its programs in 2016, to which I was asked to contribute, demanded that I ponder the political value of poetry.

The reason I recall that talk, which constitutes a small part, if a redacted one, of what ensues here, is surely that I leaned heavily on your wisdom as I brought it to shaky conclusion—on which more as I approach that very conclusion.

In Bled, I asserted that, whatever its faults, the U.S. has its virtues, and high among them, at least until lately, has been its receptiveness to immigration. This seems apt, of course, in that the only Americans who can claim to be truly indigenous are our so-called

Indians. Though I am no social scientitist, I would urge, in fact, that some other assets that America displays, or has displayed until recently—improvisatory agility, inventiveness, relative disregard for social station—owe themselves to the rich variety of cultures that the U.S. encompasses.

I think I may have inherited my positive instincts toward so-called minorities from my father, who was a liberal Republican (a species more than endangered nowadays) but who had uncommonly progressive attitudes toward what were then called racial relations. These, I know, derived from his having commanded a company of so-called "colored troops" in World War II. (Not one in ten Americans under the age of seventy could tell you that our forces were segregated until President Truman inherited the presidency.)

I barely escaped being born in Gadsden, Alabama, where my dad and his troops were stationed prior to their overseas deployment. This was directly attributable to my father's conviction, which ought to have been unexceptionable, that soldiers who would fight under his aegis should be welcome in his house. He had a group in for supper. The cross that was soon burned on my parents' lawn motivated my mother (whether at her own or her husband's instançe or both I never learned) to flee north to bear her first of five children.

How vividly I remember my incredulity, verging on contempt, at the time of the Selma march's brutalities, which pumped me full of callow fury. Dad sought to reassure me: "I won't see it in my lifetime," he said, "but you will live to see a black president." He died in 1966, young, twenty years more so than I am now. How I wish he had lived through 2008, though he would have been 99.

Or do I? The small uptick in our national polity has been followed by veiled and not so veiled racism and a hideous xenophobia. Shortly after my father's vision became reality, his own party, which an Ike-liker such as he would never recognize, elevated a knave and fool who belied its splendor.

Though that knave and fool and his followers don't know as much, there has never been a single, definable American culture. Historically, this has seemed an impediment to certain sensibilities: our lack of monarchy, aristocracy, and established religion famously drove novelist Henry James, for example, to Europe; but for others, including me, there is a hybridized glory in our most significant cultural achievements, like jazz, tap or hip-hop dancing, and even, as I have argued in various other places, much of our greatest literature. And that glory is at least partly accounted for by the multivalency of our cultural life.

It therefore greatly pains me that some portion of a nation of immigrants should now express their contempt for African America in unguarded terms, and should do so without adequate censure from our shallow commander in chief. That same faction would have us slam the door against all manner of prospective newcomers, no matter that their own surnames include the likes of O'Malley, Zukofsky, LaSalle, Belloni, and for that matter Trump. How can any of these execrate the Obamas and Bookers and Waterses of the country (not to mention the Feinsteins)? How insist on excluding people named Hernandez or Said?

America's current socio-economic problems are legion, and many angry people are now blaming them on some of the poorest and most defenseless people ever to have sought refuge on our shores. It is beyond me that such citizens should hold these struggling souls accountable for their woes, rather than faulting the obscenely wealthy, who, by way of brute economic power, have clearly been far more responsible for those woes than any other faction. Even more absurd is their imagining a Messiah in our incumbent chief executive, the very personification of what the brilliant David Bosworth calls "evangelical Mammonism."

However, to play historian or social scientist takes me out of my depth. Let me turn, therefore, to some matters about which I do know a bit, even if that knowledge itself feels tenuous too. In Slovenia, we were asked, *What can we, as writers and intellectuals, contribute to this relationship*—by which was meant that putative one between radical Islamist and western humanist—*that must grow into dialogue?* I am all for dialogue, and am far from thinking it impossible with all Islamic people, a number of whom I include among my friends. Frankly, however, I think we live in a fairy tale world if we imagine the likes of the Islamic State, Al Qaeda, Al Shabaab, or Bokol Haram to be the least interested in dialogue. Their views of the true, good, and beautiful are, it appears, absolute and non-negotiable.

Yet we were further asked, *what role must literature and culture play in raising our awareness as westerners?* Most of us are lucky enough not to live in a system such as the old USSR's, say, in which –as Joseph Brodsky once said in a journal I edited– merely to describe a flower accurately felt like a political act. But in much of the west, and certainly in the U.S, we face a subtler difficulty: namely that neither the authorities nor the public at large are likely to be swayed one way or another by anything like fiction or poetry, simply because those arts go largely unnoticed.

To that extent, our better *writing* strategies may involve newspapers or, more accurately in our day, social media, as opposed to the so-called creative arts. But even online activism, to name it that, proves problematic, for at least two reasons. The first is that social media find Einstein in the same house as the village imbecile: thus, if two disparate accounts of the same thing are broadcast, there is no determining which will strike a broad readership as more compelling. In the U.S., this was exemplified by the idiotic controversy over President Obama's birthplace. Those who chose to label him a Kenyan were simply not to be dissuaded by indisputable proof to the contrary. The social media's second great liability is that, just as oppressed parties may use them, so may their oppressors, a sad fact illustrated by the ill-starred Arab Spring and by frequent manipulations of information in China, for instance.

So it may be that more direct political activism—street demonstrations, support of genuinely progressive candidates, and so on—are the likeliest avenues to such success as progressive people may find. I am for all of these, and am and will remain a participant.

But for the sake of argument, let us imagine a literature that *was* an effective tool of change. My surmise is that, like socialist realism, it would, *qua* writing, be bad or at least tepid in any case, simply because in my view art founded primarily on an aprioristic agenda is usually doomed to inferiority.

All this may sound as though I urge political or social nonchalance upon the artist, urge him or her to be a little Nero, playing the violin as Rome burns. Not at all. In fact, exactly the contrary. Any poet who stayed innocent of the great migrant crisis would be no poet at all. An artist must be as open as possible to all manner of observation, and must be jealous of those observatory powers, because the threats to them are myriad. To allow that openness to be usurped by *anything*—even the noblest political or moral conviction—is by my lights suicidal.

Here is a remark of your own, estimable Fleda, which resonates with me, and which I used at the P.E.N. colloquy:

> I've long since quit worrying about whether writing itself is a worthy use of my life. Whether it is or isn't doesn't change my inclination to do it. Anyway, I'm positive that it matters, words themselves being small bulbs buried under the soil, small grenades.

I hope to my God that you're right, but in any case, I know that a willful effort to make my poems "political" or "relevant" will serve no one: not me, not my reader, and not the causes I passionately subscribe to, including a sane and compassionate attitude toward those disrupted by violence, along with the development of a non-hysterical stance toward terrorism.

The only thing I really know to do in my role as artist is to beat at my keyboard. If what results is an explosion, I must accept that. If I am moved by a bloom or a bird or the birth of a grandchild, these are what I need to bring forth. The point is, we writers need to sustain belief in our own voices, and in their autonomy—not to the point of perversity or narcissism, but right up *to* those points. If we allow our voices to be controlled by dogma, even virtuous dogma (if there be such a thing), we might as well be writing advertisements or propaganda. We need to believe that our sincerest testimonies matter, even if we cannot define how that may be in any definitive way. We need to agree with American poet William Carlos William's assertion that

It is difficult
to get the news from poems
yet men die miserably every day
     for lack
of what is found there.

And again I agree with you, Fleda:

> Okay, to be really blunt: What do I—as a writer—do about Donald Trump? Theodore Roethke said, "My heart keeps open house." Omit nothing. Bombs, bullets, butterflies, beetles, Trump.

With such encouragement in mind, I composed something that's as "political" as I'm apt ever to offer:

Worries

I have a very dear friend whose anxieties
Merge the big and small. Our political life,
Needless to say, but her plumbing too, or the dicey
State of a shop she fears will not survive

For lack of custom in her tidy Midwest town.
I recently had the nerve to chide this friend
For her copious worries, despite my copious own.
For example, this morning I drove through a nasty blend

Of rain and snow to the village, where my stomach churned:
I spotted our local roofer up on a scaffold
Against a house. Too risky. And yet the world
Wasn't ending, and isn't. Not every last thing's awful

Or new. We've always had monsters, say, like the one
From Cleveland, who lately posted videos
Of himself on YouTube as he killed some random old man.
But since human beings drew breath there've been evil and woe.

What's so patently different nowadays is that nothing
Is hidden, off limits, not even the raves of morons
Who voice their opinions online, like the ones insisting
That Mr. Obama's a Kenyan, his family all Muslims.

Our screen world plops the village idiot down
At the very same keyboard as a modern-day Aristotle's.
Viewers can choose the claim that turns them on.
When a newer president spoke of a terrorist horror

In Sweden, for instance, its nonexistence seemed
To his backers non-important. My friend? She frets
Too much, but for whatever it's worth I understand.
I didn't see that roofer today when I passed.

What happened to him? I'd come to pick up the paper,
Which of course was filled . . . well, I'll spare you platitude.
I suppose somehow the shopkeepers, roofers and plumbers
Will endure, while other matters, understood

Or vague, are apter to lead us into disaster.
As for me, I'm chiefly worried, despite my preachments,
That these days there aren't enough like my friend who get it,
Though what is *it?* Dear reader, let's just be persistent,

Since this stuff will break your fucking heart if you let it.

RE: POLITICS

Fleda: Politics

WE'VE WRITTEN ABOUT becoming poets, but we haven't written about remaining poets, have we? Remaining when suddenly the world seems determined to blow itself apart, and our democracy is perilously frayed at the seams. Are we the same poets as before? Will there necessarily be a yawning gulf between our past remembrances and what we say now?

World events are already bleeding heavily into my poems. But that doesn't negate the personal history, the Life in Poetry the present is built upon. In fact, my personal past—the objects, the people, the events—take on a glow, a revelatory quality. This is life, this is authentic life, this is True. One particular life matters.

⊷

When I was in the second grade, Ike Eisenhower ran for President against Adlai Stevenson. Ike was a huge popular favorite, a smiling guy, and a General to boot. Fear of Communism was at an all-time high. The slogan was "I'd rather be Dead than Red." Surely it was a good idea to "Like Ike," as the buttons said, rather than take a chance on the somewhat dour intellectual Adlai Stevenson. My parents, though, were voting for Stevenson. So of course I was for him, too. My first memory of asserting myself politically was the embarrassment and pain of standing in the schoolyard while my friends chanted "She'd rather be Red than Dead!" the counter-slogan of Ike's supporters.

My mother's father, a Missourian, was a life-long Democrat. I still have a letter that Harry Truman wrote him, thanking him for his support. One of the great events of his life was shaking hands with the great man. His daughter, my mother, didn't follow the news very closely and couldn't have told you why she voted as she did, in any election, but it was clear she resolutely voted the way her father did, because she adored him.

My mother's values were, as is true of many others, formed at an early age and didn't change much. For instance, she was schooled to think Blacks inferior and pretty much held on to that opinion. She was a kind, gentle woman, more conservative than her husband and children. I believe in her latter years, her vote often defied my father's, and mine. She voted for Nixon, I know. She wasn't articulate or knowledgeable enough to out-argue us, so she mostly kept quiet. She voted with what she thought her heart told her.

My father was an economist, and inclined to see politics in terms of gross national debt. It's interesting to watch him now, at 99, struggle to understand our president. He can't conceive of such a level of lying and self-interest. He's occasionally swayed by the conservative views of his caretakers, but he keeps struggling to see beyond the walls of his small room, where he's mostly confined.

Truthfully, I can't remember much political talk in my family, with so much else to be worried about. I have not had a natural inclination toward politics. Which is to say, my efforts have generally been concentrated closer to home, on staying emotionally afloat, myself. Also, later, as a grad student, when it came to poetry, I was schooled in New Criticism, that preached examining creative work from within its own boundaries, not looking at context for meaning. The other side of that thinking was that good poetry ought to look inward, that the private self is the source of the poem, and that a "political" poem is way too "public like a frog," and generally bad, to boot. As evidence, anyone could cite Edna St. Vincent Millay's poems from the '30s. Pure propaganda.

The current political climate, though, has been a slap in the face to me. Wham, I've entered a new consciousness. Not just me. It looks as if American poets have finally joined their counterparts in other countries who articulate their struggles within a political context.

In all my years of writing, I have never before been compelled to scrutinize so closely my need to write. I have never before examined the word "selfish" with such disinterest. Self-ish. Belonging to, having the characteristics of the self. Overly concerned with self. How much is "overly?" Is it my "self" that I'm so concerned with as a writer?

Dunno. I have asked myself what I need to do, politically. I've written what letters I felt compelled to write to our elected officials. I've closely followed the news. Even as I'm getting to the age when the lyric impulse generally is thought to wane, there seems to be more passion than ever in my poems, no matter the subject. I feel a stronger sense of audience. Not to change minds, but to embody— to witness—life as it comes through me, somehow.

As poets age, I notice that often the poems begin to loosen, relax, and speak more quietly. The voice is often more confident, and the subjects more inclusive of all surroundings. This might be true regardless of the political catastrophe of late. It's odd. Even though the energy—call it passion—in my poems feels stronger to me, the voice seems to grown calmer, confident, not of my particular ability, but of the right to speak. I guess that's it.

I sent you a recent poem of mine called "The Temple Frog." You praised it, so I'll use it here. It begins this way:

> The albino African frog may or may not be alive, it is so
> still. It hangs there under water, a gelatinous suspension.
>
> I pretend it isn't ugly since the monks keep it, feed it, but
> it's like a fat pale blob squeezed in my diaphragm
>
> that I can't cough up. It knows nothing except encasement.

It is very religious that way, I think, not worrying about

death and equanimous about the other side of the tank.
Then there it goes, a slick swoosh with its webbed toes,

sliding its stomach over the one prominent rock, both
fortress and hiding. I have lived into this millennium

in which a frog can torment me this way! . . . . . .

The poem ends like this:

It is the year 2017, and everything has changed out here.

Sorrow's streaming through the window. What is time,
then? What is a lifetime at Abu Ghraib, Guantanamo?

What is a lifetime spent in passionate prayer? What, when
the vastness has left us only this small space to use?

This is overtly political, right? It comes from the same close
examination of the world that has always fed into my poems, but its
outward expanse feels newly explosive to me.

Basically, I think the greatest threat to my work would be to cease
concentrating on the writing itself because I feel guilty—because
I feel that I "ought" to be making more dramatic gestures. To get
caught up in obsessively watching political videos where like-
minded people console me in our mutual horror. To get the jitters.
To give in to panic and/or despair.

Stick with the frog poems, on the whole, I repeat to myself.

I'd say the times require a monastic discipline. The hard work of
overt persistent resistance needs to be done, but so does the hard
work of doing nothing. As you know, I've been a meditator for
almost 30 years. Why I would sit and stare at the wall every morning

is a source of wonderment to some friends. This practice, however, is exactly analogous to the writing life. There must be silence. There must be a growing awareness of space around events. Not that action is not important, but that Velcro-ing ourselves onto attitudes hinders clear vision. What we write needs to come from silence, needs to open itself into silence, not hostage to anything.

I just turned 73. Politics, of course, have been swirling around me all of my life, whether I was bent out of shape by events or not. I think of my aging, and of my poems, as a gradual opening up to more and more of what was there all along—the brightness, the awfulness, the joy, the grief—the whole complex mess of existence. The more open the poems are, the more energy they take in, the more they are able to radiate. I hope that's true.

CPSIA information can be obtained
at www.ICGtesting.com
Printed in the USA
LVHW020141061118
596065LV00004B/4/P